LEAN START-UP, LEAN ENTERPRISE AND ANALYTICS

3 BOOKS IN 1

TABLE OF CONTENTS

WHAT IS LEAN START-UP?

A lean start-up is a technique utilized to found a new firm or present a new item in support of an existing business. The lean start-up technique supporters developing products that consumers have currently demonstrated they want so that a market will already exist as quickly as the product is introduced. As opposed to creating an item and afterward hoping that demand will emerge. Lean start-up is a strategy for developing new companies based upon the belief that entrepreneurs have to examine, experiment and iterate as they establish items.

The idea of lean start-up came from the very early 2000s and advanced into an approach around 2010. It was created by Silicon Valley entrepreneurs Steve Space and Eric Ries and advertised by early adopters consisting of Share through co-founder and CTO Rob Fan.

Lean start-up vs. typical start-up strategies

The concepts within a lean start-up contradict long-held principles regarding how entrepreneurs must approach launching a brand-new service. Conventional thoughts imply that business owners should develop a multiyear service plan and afterward use that strategy to raise money to fund item development activities. Standard concepts advise entrepreneurs to create their product in a "stealth setting," thus keeping their item ideas unknown to any individual beyond the start-up workers and their financiers. The lean start-up approach requires business owners to start their organization ventures by looking for company design and, after that evaluating their ideas. Comments from prospective clients are then made use of to readjust their ideas as they move on.

Qualities

The lean start-up method also supports for entrepreneurs to consistently participate in this task loop-- exploring and developing theories that they then check amongst customers to generate comments, something referred to as validated knowing. Business owners utilize consumer comments to re-engineer their products. Lean start-up advocates for repetitive, or active, advancement ideas adjusted from the world of software advancement.

A lean start-up will build a prototype quickly, get it to market to gauge the success of the item without expending unnecessary sources, and use the information generated by early advertising examinations to influence the following construct stage. In lean production, this method is called kaizen. In programming, the method is called Agile. Furthermore, the lean start-up approach asks for business owners to establish a minimal practical item or MVP that they can test. These supporters for business owners to adjust their items based upon consumer feedback--

another key idea of the approach that is called "pivoting."

The Lean start-up technique was an instant hit in Silicon Valley, as start-ups welcomed this brand-new speculative principle. The technique showed to be a fairly easy educational tool, so it became a mainstay of start-up accelerators and entrepreneurship classes anywhere. Lean Start-ups were not the only big adjustment in the start-up approach of the last ten years, as one more, quieter revolution was occurring. Fortunately the evidence recommends that start-ups should take part in trial and error along the lines originated by the Lean start-up Method.

A team of Italian academics carried out a gold-standard randomized controlled experiment on 116 start-ups. Half of them were shown how to do extensive experiments on their start-up ideas, creating theories, and evaluating them systematically. The others were educated to do experiments yet were not shown how to utilize the clinical technique of hypothesis generation. The groups that imitated scientists did far better-- rotating much more, staying clear of problems, and eventually creating greater profits than the control team. Rigorous testing is clearly essential to start-up success. However, various other job has shown that there are elements of the Lean Start- up Method that may, in fact, be damaging. In a brand-new paper, a team of popular entrepreneurship scholars recognized two major issues with the method.

Lean Start-ups push you to "leave the office" and speak with clients as quickly as feasible. They concentrate on obtaining fast comments from clients to very little viable products makes start-ups vulnerable to go for step-by-step renovations, focusing on what customers want today, rather than trying to see ahead into the future. Looking for exterior validation from early clients can thus be even harder if you have an innovation concept than if you have a step-by-step, and a convenient explanation for. This trouble is compounded by the Company Version Canvas. While the inquiries the Canvas asks work, you should recognize that your consumers are. What is your theory regarding the world based on your distinct expertise and beliefs?

Completing the nine boxes of the Canvas rather focuses you on what your start-up looks like at the end of the process-- when you have the sophisticated channel and supplier relationships, and so forth-- yet there is no roadmap to get to that end-state in the Lean start-up Method. The detailed service components of the Canvas unknown the actual insights that make your idea unique.

What does it really mean to be a lean start-up?

Advocates of the methodology claim lean start-up principles make certain that business owners develop products that customers actually want, rather than trying to develop organizations based upon untested ideas. Supporters describe this way of thinking as "fall short fast, fall short inexpensive" since the lean start-up procedure is designed to restrict the moment and cash purchased product suggestions prior to entrepreneurs have to examine and prove their prospective value.

History of the technique

Numerous publications aided popularize lean start-up concepts. One of the most identified is Ries' 2011 book The Lean Start-up. Ries that had researched a customer advancement training course shown by Blank in the very early 2000s after Blank had actually purchased his start-up attracted inspiration from Toyota's agile strategy to making known as lean manufacturing.

Gaging Customer Interest

By using lean start-up principles, item developers can gauge consumer passion in the product and establish just how the item may need to be refined. This process is called verified discovery, and it can be utilized to prevent the unnecessary use of sources in product production and growth. Through lean start-up, if an idea is likely to stop working, it will stop working rapidly and cheaply as opposed to slowly and expensively, for this reason, the term "fail- fast."

Lean Start-up and advance business

The lean start-up technique separates itself from the traditional company version when it pertains to hiring. Lean start-ups work with employees that can learn, adapt, and job swiftly while standard services work with employees based on experience and ability.

Lean start-ups use various financial coverage metrics; rather than focusing on revenue declarations, annual reports, and capital statements, they focus on client acquisition expense, lifetime consumer value, consumer spin price, and just how viral their product could be.

Needs for Lean Start-up

The lean start-up technique takes into consideration testing to be better than any detailed preparation. Five-year business plans constructed around unknowns are thought-about a waste of time, and client response is critical. As opposed to service plans, lean start-ups use an organization version based upon hypotheses that are examined rapidly. The information does not need to be finished before continuing; it simply requires to be enough. When customers do not respond as desired, the start-up promptly adjusts to limit its losses and return to establishing products consumers' desire. Failure is the mother of success.

Entrepreneurs following this approach test their hypotheses by engaging with prospective clients, buyers, and partners to assess their reactions about product features, pricing, circulation, and client purchase. With the details, entrepreneurs make small changes called iterations to products, and large adjustments called pivots to fix any kind of major worries. This screening phase might lead to transforming the target customer or changing the product to better offer the present target client.

The lean start-up technique first recognizes trouble that needs to be addressed. It then establishes a minimum viable item or the smallest form of the product that permits business owners to present it to possible clients for comments. This technique is very efficient and fast and less expensive than developing the final product for testing and decreases the threat that start-ups encounter by reducing their high failure rate drastically. The lean start-up also redefines a start-up as an organization that is looking for a scalable organization version, not one that has an existing company plan that it is established to carry out.

Instance of Lean Start-up

For instance, a healthy meal shipment solution that is targeting busy, solitary 20-somethings in metropolitan areas may learn that it has a far better market in 30-something affluent mothers of infants in the residential areas. The business may then alter its distribution schedule and the kinds of foods it offers to provide the ideal nutrition for brand-new mommies. It could also add options for dishes for spouses or companions and other kids in the home.

The lean start-up technique is not to be made use of solely by start-ups. Firms such as General Electric, Qualcomm, and Intuit have all used the lean start-up technique; GE used the approach to develop a new battery for use by mobile phone companies in establishing nations where electrical energy is undependable.

METHODOLOGY OF LEARN START-UP

The Lean start-up supplies a scientific technique for creating and taking care of start-ups and get a wanted item to customers' hands faster. The Lean start-up method educates you just how to drive a start-up-how to guide, when to turn back, and when to persevere-and grow an organization with optimum acceleration. It is a principled strategy for new item advancement. Several start-ups begin with a concept for a product that they think people desire. Then after that, they invest months, often years, developing that product without ever revealing the product, also in a very rudimentary form, to the potential consumer. When they fall short to get to a broad uptake from consumers, it is usually due to the fact that they never talked with possible clients and determined whether or not the item was something they were genuinely interested in or had use for. When consumers eventually communicate, with their indifference, that they uncommitted about the idea, the start-up fails.

Eliminate Unpredictability

The absence of a customized administration procedure has led numerous a start-up or, as Ries terms them, "a human institution designed to produce a brand-new product and services under conditions of extreme unpredictability," to desert all process. They take a "just do it" strategy that prevents all kinds of management. Using the Lean Start-up strategy, a business can produce order, not turmoil, by supplying tools to examine a vision continuously. Lean doesn't just concern investing much less cash. Lean isn't almost failing quick, stopping work inexpensively. It is about placing a procedure, an approach around the advancement of a product.

Work Smarter Not Harder

The Lean Start-up method has as a premise that every start-up is a grand experiment that tries to address a concern. The inquiry is not, "Can this product be built?" Instead, the concerns are "Should this item be built?" and "Can we develop a lasting organization around this collection of services and products?" This experiment is more than simply theoretical inquiry; it is the first item. If it is successful, it permits a manager to get going with their campaign: getting very early adopters, adding employees to every additional experiment or model, and ultimately beginning to develop an item. At that exact time, that product is ready to be dispersed commonly, and it will have established clients. It will have fixed real troubles and supply comprehensive specifications wherefore needs to be constructed.

1. Entrepreneurs Are All-over

In the times past, we understand that most big businesses began in a garage and functioned there and were called start-ups. However, today start-ups are not a small time operation out of a garage. What you must learn from this concept is that there has never been a much better time to introduce your concept than today. Think big. Begin Small. Scale Rapid. That is the mentality behind this principle. If you have a concept, begin small in your bedroom or any place, then keep going.

2. Entrepreneurship is Administration

This 2nd principle is based upon the institutionalizing of a start-up. Start-ups are not just products. Start-ups are organizations that show you exactly how to handle your organization. It warrants consequently that every start-up is different from the various other. That proves that the techniques of managing start-ups today have to be geared in the direction of the context. You need to handle your start-up in a manner that the techniques are tailored for your start-up.

3. Validated Understanding

The Lean Start-up is based upon a knowing process. The learning component is a legitimate way of building your company. The proven assumption is that if you hang the development of your product on what the customers want, constantly and diligently, you will certainly most absolutely never fail on the end product that comes after the process.

4. Technology Audit

In a start-up, accountancy degrees won't simply be financial-based recording earnings, losses, earnings, and sales, and they will certainly also entail what the Lean Start-up refers to as "the boring stuff" like just how to determine development, just how to arrangement landmarks, exactly how to prioritize job. This sort of accountancy is called innovation accountancy. Make up the creative ways you are generating in your start-up to fix troubles. This will be essential since it holds the entrepreneurs answerable, specifically when they are bootstrapping and have no financiers.

Establish an MVP

A core element of the Lean Start-up method is the build-measure-learn feedback loophole. The primary step is identifying the trouble that needs to be fixed and, after that creating a minimum sensible item (MVP) to begin the procedure of discovering as rapidly as possible. Once the MVP is established, a start-up can deal with adjusting the engine. This will include dimension and understanding; and need to consist of workable metrics that can show cause and effect inquiry. The start-up will use an investigatory growth approach called the "Five Whys"- asking straightforward concerns to study and resolve issues in the process. When this process of determining and learning is done properly, it will be clear that a company is either moving the chauffeurs of the business model or not. Otherwise, it is a sign that it is time to pivot or make an architectural program improvement to check a new fundamental hypothesis about the item, method and engine of growth.

1.   **Establish the baseline**

You can run an MVP test to establish some benchmark information factors. This could involve a smoke test, with pure marketing, simply to see if their passion from possible customers. It might entail a sign-up type online to see if clients would purchase a product and services.

2.   **Tuning the Engine**

With the standard developed, the next step is to make a single change that can be tested to surpass it. Rather than making many changes all at once, concentrate on one point. This could be the layout of the signup kind; does it boost the number of conversions? Tuning the engine must be done meticulously by checking one hypothesis each time.

3.   Pivot or Persevere

After making a number of iterations via the cycle, you must be moving up from the baseline in the direction of the suitable goal laid out in the business strategy. If this is not happening, it needs to be noticeable as a result of the incremental learning actions taken along the way.

4. Learn, Build and Measure

It can be the main point. The procedure of constructing a huge firm is hard. This basic principle will serve as guidance for you as an entrepreneur to build your minimum viable product (MVP) after that construct your big business around this MVP tweaking and adjusting around it. Prior to adjusting, you must evaluate the effects and metrics from individuals using the item and the market. For you to add everything up to a total, it is a process of construct first, gauge the item's impacts to consumers and the marketplace, then find out and develop once again each and every single time taking into consideration the metrics you measured.

If there is one idea that has changed the methods, we seek advancement today greater than any other, it's the concept of using the clinical method to take care of unpredictability. This means defining a hypothesis, developing a tiny item or feature which can check that theory, after that discover what happens, and readjust accordingly. This easy technique is showing tremendous results and allows firms to make small bank on lots of suggestions simultaneously and permit the findings to establish which ideas relocate through evictions.

Build-Measure-Learn can be put on practically anything, not simply brand- new items. You can evaluate a customer support concept, an administration testimonial procedure, site message, and deals, or a new feature to an existing product. It's important that you can plainly test and validate the theory, though - you need to be able to collect sufficient information or metrics to measure the results of the build. The goal is to locate the quickest way to repeat through the Build-Measure-Learn cycle. You'll want to figure out whether it deserves another cycle, or to quit and go on to an additional concept. This indicates specifying an extremely certain suggestion to examination, and minimum products to gauge. With products, you're aiming to examine whether clients, in fact, want or require it.

6. The Pivot

Deciding to pivot is among the hardest aspects of the Lean start-up method, due to the fact that creators and business owners are psychologically connected to their items, energy and cash have actually been ploughed into them. Some difficulties do arise, such as vanity metrics and not testing the best hypothesis can lead teams down the wrong course. If the theory isn't clear, after that failing can seem evasive, because you don't understand with the assurance that this undertaking isn't functioning. "Launch it and see what takes place" always causes a positive result: you will indeed see what happens!

A pivot is not necessarily a failing, and it means that you will certainly alter one of the fundamental theories that you began with. There are different variations on the pivot:

- **Zoom-in pivot.** A single function in the item now becomes the entire product.
- **Zoom-out pivot.** The opposite of the above. An entire product comes to be a solitary function in something a lot bigger.
- **Consumer sector pivot.** The product was right, yet the original consumer sector wasn't altering to a various customer is needed, but the item remains the exact same. Customer need pivot. With confirmed discovering, it becomes clear that more important trouble requires to be resolved for the customer than the original.

- **Platform pivot**. Usually, platforms start out as an application, yet due to success, it grows to become a platform environment.
- **Organization architecture pivot**. Changing how value is recorded basically modifications whatever else in business (advertising strategy, expense structure, product, etc.). The engine of development pivot. Start-ups generally follow among viral, sticky, or paid development models, according to Ries. Altering from one to the other may be required to fuel faster development.
- **Network pivot** - The internet has created many more channel options for start-ups, and complex sales or advertising and marketing networks are far less dominant. A start-up has many more choices from the get-go. Technology pivot. New modern technology can use considerable advantages in

expense, performance, or efficiency, and allow you to keep everything else the exact same.

7. Small Sets

The story goes that a man needs to pack e-newsletters into envelopes with the help of his two children. The children recommend they initially fold all the e-newsletters, then placed stamps on every letter, then write the address - do every job one at a time.

The dad intended to do it in different ways, finishing every envelope totally prior to moving onto the next. They contended to see which approach was much faster. The dad's technique won, as a result of the method called "single-piece circulation," typically used in lean manufacturing. It appears far more effective to replicate the exact same work over and over given that we presume we'll get better and quicker at it as we go. Yet private efficiency is not as critical as the general effectiveness of the system. Time is shed between the 'sets' when you need to restack the letters and prepare the envelopes.

8. The Andon Cord

As simply pointed out, the Andon Cord was made use of by Toyota to enable any employee along the assembly line to call a halt to the system if an issue was uncovered. The longer a problem continues along with the manufacturing, the tougher and a lot more costly it is to get rid of. Detecting an issue promptly is highly efficient, even if it implies stopping the whole production line up until it's addressed.

Eric Ries clarifies that at IMVU, they applied a comprehensive **collection of automatic** checks which ran each day. They would certainly guarantee the standard operations of the website (such as an 'acquisition' button) still operated. This meant that any production mistakes were caught promptly and immediately, and no more changes were taken into manufacturing until it was resolved. It was the shows matching of the Andon cable.

9. Constant Implementation

For some, it may appear a little dated in 2016, provided the standardization of SaaS applications, but for numerous, continual deployment is a terrifying and unbelievable situation. The suggestion is that you are regularly updating your real-time production systems, all day, every day. This was feasible because a considerable investment into test scripts - around 15,000 examination manuscripts would certainly run over 70 times a day, imitating everything from individual clicks the internet browser, to running back-end code in the database.

10. Kanban

Kanban is another strategy obtained from the lean manufacturing globe. Ries offers an example from Grockit (an online skills enhancement tool for standardized tests). Grockit produces 'tales' in their item advancement procedure; stories are created to build an attribute; they include what the advantage and end result is for the end customer. These tales are after that verified to see if they work - a split test is used to confirm the renovation to the client experience.

Kanban has four states:

-     Backlog - things which are ready to be worked with, yet have actually not yet started
-     Underway - things currently undergrowth
-     Constructed - growth has actually finished work on the item, it awaits the consumer
-     Verified - thing has actually been launched, and it's been positively confirmed.

If the tale failed the recognition test, it would certainly be eliminated from the product.

An excellent practice is to set that none of the four phases (pails) can include more than three jobs at any type of once. If a job has been developed, it cannot move right into the confirmed stage until there is space for it (less than three currently in there). Similarly, work cannot begin on stockpile things till the underway bucket frees up. An extremely useful result of using this technique is that groups begin to gauge their efficiency according to the confirmed knowing from the customer, and not the amount of brand-new functions generated.

11. The 5 Whys

The majority of technical issues have, at their origin, a human reason. Using the five whys method allows you to get closer to that origin. It's deceptively easy, yet extremely effective, and Eric Ries thinks most troubles which are discovered tend to come from the absence of ideal training - but on the surface either resemble a technical problem or private person's error.

As an instance, Ries supplies a situation from IMVU where customers were whining regarding a recent item upgrade:

- A brand-new release disabled an attribute for

consumers. Why? Since a specific server failed.

- Why did the webserver fail? Since an obscure subsystem was utilized in the wrong method.
- The designer that utilized it really did not know just how to use it properly.
- Why didn't he understand? Since he was never educated.
- Why wasn't he educated? Since his supervisor doesn't count on training new engineers because he and his group are "also busy.

The method is specifically valuable for start-ups, as it enables them to find the optimal speed for making improvements. You could spend a massive quantity in training, yet it might not be the optimal thing to do at that stage of growth - yet by looking at origin to issues, you can recognize whether there are core areas that need focus, and not just always concentrate on the surface concerns. We also often tend to overreact to things that take place in the moment, and the 5 Whys helps us to take a deeper take look at what is truly taking place.

There can be a propensity to make use of the 5 Whys as the Five Blames in the beginning, with team members aiming to claim who was at fault for each action. The main objectives of the Five Whys are to find persistent troubles brought on by poor process, and tolerable people. It is crucial that everybody remains in the room together when the evaluation is done; all of the individuals influenced by the concern (including monitoring and customer support reps). When blame needs to be taken, it is a very important administration (or the Chief Executive Officer) takes the pinch-hit not having a system-level service in place to stop the concern.

Excellent methods for beginning with the 5 Whys:

Mutual dependence on and empowerment. Be forgiving of all errors the very first time; never ever enable the same blunder to be made twice. Most blunders are as a result of a flawed system, maintain people concentrated on resolving problems at that degree.

Face undesirable truths. The method is most likely to surface unpleasant realities regarding the firm, and the effort to take care of those very early tough issues is going to be considerable. It can easily become the Five Blames. This is where elderly management buy-in is vital to serve as umpire, making sure that the process is complied with.

Beginning little, specify. You wish to obtain the process embedded, so begin with tiny issues, with tiny remedies. Focus on running the process regularly, including as many people as you can.

Select a Five Whys master. This person is the main adjustment agent, so they require to have a good degree of authority to get points done.

Where the lean start-up radiates

One of the most effective recognized and most effective supporters of the lean start-up design is Dropbox. The common cloud storage app expanded extremely swiftly in a highly-saturated market, and Chief Executive Officer Drew Houston credit scores a lot of that energy to the application of Eric Ries' lean start-up concepts. Houston has actually given that created and spoken thoroughly on the subject. Assessing his run-through of exactly how Dropbox efficiently went lean describes the generally accepted benefits of lean start-up ideas:

Minimum sensible product (MVP)

The initial exclusive "launch" of Dropbox was really absolutely nothing of the type. At the time, Houston and a couple of good friends had a fleshed-out idea, a barebones model primarily coded, and an ambitious growth calendar, yet little else. With just those assets in hand, Houston began reaching out to prospective capitalists and customers with a simple combination of videos and a touchdown page for collecting email addresses.

This illustrates the core lean start-up principle of the minimal practical product Dropbox was able to attain powerful traction, funding, and a ton of useful comments based on an application that was not even finished yet. Rather, it had a model that was sufficient for highlighting its objectives, and an ambitious development roadmap that financiers and users both can support. Focusing on establishing an MVP permits lean start-ups to go to market, discover, and repeat extra quickly than start-ups that concentrate on establishing a brightened, completed item first and foremost. This loophole lets them rapidly respond to one of the most crucial questions for every single start-up: "Is this an item individuals are willing to spend for?"

Client development

A crucial tenet of the lean start-up method is actually obtained-- with all proper attribution-- from another keen service mind of the early 21st century, Steve Space, and his concept of consumer growth. While there's much more to the total concept, the overarching point is that "construct it and they will certainly come" virtually never works, and entrepreneurs who depend on that concept are misleading themselves. Instead, start-ups require to approach the advancement of their consumer base or target market is equally as extensive and disciplined a fashion as they come close to item growth, quality assurance, and marketing.

In Dropbox's situation, these concepts reverberated with Houston, and he recognized early that he and his founders were, themselves, early tech adopters. This was a consumer character they knew well and recognized. They were, consequently, able to target various other early adopters with laser accuracy in the means they created and distributed those first videos and numerous various other items of material that complied with. The outcome of this disciplined, targeted growth of its client base was quick fostering and successful development in the neighbourhood of 15 to 20 percent, month-over-month for many years.

Believing artistically

Ultimately, the lean start-up design's concentrate on regularly trying out, keeping an eye on and iterating based upon results brings about a typical outcome: Firms find that a number of the standard marketing and growth techniques they really felt forced to carry out because "that's simply exactly how you do it" didn't work. On the other hand, assuming outside packages and attempting something brand-new commonly led to unforeseen success. As it drew near a complete public launch, Dropbox invested heavily in SEO and

SEM because that's what all its competitors were doing.

Maintaining a close eye on analytics showed that these approaches were supplying a terrible price of acquisition-- over $300 per consumer. With some creative thinking, nevertheless, the business recognized that much of its ongoing development was due to completely satisfied customers routinely telling pals concerning the application. Dropbox decided to urge these habits by establishing its now-iconic referral program-- invite a close friend to Dropbox, and you both obtain 250 megabytes of bonus storage space as they say, is the background.

WHAT'S THE FUTURE OF LEAN START-UPS?

While there's no refuting that several firms have actually seen wonderful success adhering to Eric Ries' guidelines for lean start-ups, the method has its movie critics as well. By the author's own admission, it's not a formula for success in all situations or markets. Nevertheless, especially in the United States and industries that support local business, also ten years into the lean start-up activity, the majority of the lustre stays. The principles and guidelines simply operate in lots of cases.

Is it reasonable to expect lean start-ups to remain to succeed moving forward? There's no factor to believe or else. The secret is for each business owner to inform themselves on lean principles as one of the various methods to start-up success. After that, via cautious planning and experimentation, determine what's most likely to work best for bringing their unique vision to life.

The Lean Connection

Being "lean" in this situation describes creating the cheapest, fastest experiments you can handle, in order to test the core property of your project with time. In other words, every sprint and every story remains in some method an experiment, which will ostensibly give useful brand-new information to guide your recurring prioritization and stockpile evolution.

The Enterprise Angle

Any kind of business getting in a brand-new particular niche, whether developed or otherwise, must discover brand-new points in order to strategy and manage effectively. The Lean start-up process focuses on minimizing the numerous dangers that arise throughout any type of brand-new product development effort, such as:

- Are we addressing genuine, considerable troubles?
- Who specifically has these troubles, and would our recommended option be great enough that they would certainly pay a beneficial price for it?
- Is there any type of technological threats that we need to tease out and deal with?

Offered then that the requirement for development and transparent danger management can be just as essential in a big organization as in a tiny one, where are a few usual locations of effect and problem?

Profile monitoring-- The Lean start-up provides measurable methods to gauge development against certain goals, giving guidance on when to "pivot" (adjustment direction), invest more, or quit jobs. Rapid shipments imply tighter responses loops, which implies different PMO structures and tempos, for example.

Resource monitoring-- As with agile approaches, establishing and managing lasting dedicated teams is fairly different from the norm for several firms. Appropriate equilibrium of practical management and skills development with cross-functional groups is a need.

Brand name monitoring-- Much less of a concern for start-ups is the opportunity of credibility damages from short fallen experiments. Large companies might utilize spin-off brand names, or high target quality constricted accessibility launches just too very early adopters, keeping in mind the pilot nature of the projects.

Quality monitoring-- The "Minimum Viable Product" launch strategy preferred by the Lean Start-up motion is usually implied to be a high-quality compromise. This demand does not hold true; as with dexterous, the emphasis is on simply developing a few functions each time (enough to satisfy some actual requirement) but crafting them well. Regulatory factors to consider and the like need to be addressed freely and drive the "meaning of done" as ideal.

Applying It to Your Business

Most businesses operate in lean, nimble, falls, or a cocktail of the three for software program development, and we all may have experienced some kind of them as an Experience (UI/UX) Designer. Lean start-up is a product development method started by Eric Ries in 2008 and promoted by his book released in 2011.

Eric incorporated the best of nimble and lean techniques based upon his experience and developed this method. Lean start-up is not new to the start-up globe but is progressively being utilized at ventures that want to innovate around their consumers. Lean Start-up at a business relocates R&D experiments in the hands of their customers, making use of a very little practical item (MVP). This brings an item to market faster and cheaper with verified understandings while iterating and regularly releasing in extremely brief cycles.

Technology is always tough in a business environment. I lately invested a year dealing with a large company on a project that looked to get rid of the technology obstacle by applying the Lean Start-up method. The job objective was to improve retail client experience by creating an online offering for an existing offline item-- one with reputable consumers and earnings. From my point of view as an Experience Design expert, the executive-level choice to "utilize Lean Start-up" was a strong move with lots of benefits. However, it was not without hiccups.

Lesson 1: Prepare your team.

Offering alignment to do this methodology is vital, and our group started with very little. In our initial Lean start-up workshop, a lean coach introduced himself, provided a little brief, and we started our sprint. Mid-sprint, a few designers, shared their concern around on-boarding the idea of throw- away code if invalidated by users after the week ended two developers left strangely.

Lesson 2: Obtain constant support from a Lean start-up professional.

Unfortunately, lean coach was unavailable after a week. We were anticipated to read the Lean Start-up publication, self-organize, establish an MVP, and iterate. This was a skilled group, yet it was difficult to straddle between old product advancement routines and new. For a new procedure like this, some regular expert guidance was required. It took our team a month to understand that a lean coach was called for on a regular basis.

Lesson 3: Construct a separate sandbox for lean start-up projects.

It took designers nearly six months to figure out just how to develop an MVP beyond normal Dev-environment. The existing environment supported bi-monthly releases, and it was hard to launch anything beyond these cycles. Our executives wanted a rapid method of developing a product that by-passed usual company procedures. He was extremely dynamic; however, the Dev- team was so nervous about making points outside the standard since it could jeopardize security. The team was relieved, and we might deploy quicker, leveraging the company's infrastructure.

Lesson 4: It's not about the excellent quality layout; it has to do with the item.

I assumed I would go back to my common process of making illustrations, do some alternatives, cords, add visuals, obtain material strategists entailed, testimonial with principals and directors, do a couple of versions and then send them for advancement after authorizations. Thankfully, my style supervisor was at lean coaching, and she got this methodology. I was worried about endangering design, and she described just how it's not about the quality. Testing and confirming ideas preceded, then came top quality once they had actually been validated. It took some time to adjust to this way of functioning; however, making hi-fidelity designs based upon confirmed understandings is quite amazing. I might think about extra delightful details while observing validation sessions. The initial item was constructed of whiteboards sketches, with very little layout information. This happened for an initial couple of experiments after that moving to medium-fidelity, and the quality kept enhancing. At later stages, we were iterating with hi-fidelity designs as those assets got developed.

Lesson 5: MVP can be perplexed with a PoC, Mock, or a model.

Whatever fidelity we made was last and all set to be before customers. It either stayed, advanced, or was gotten rid of. All phases see the light of day and do genuine service. You can state that it is a pilot; it collaborated with some people that really did not obtain the idea of an MVP. It's very easy to merge a proof of idea (PoC), simulated, or a prototype with MVP. It's none of those, PoC collects hints of evidence concerning the importance of a suggestion, simulated is for stakeholders to see the vision revived aesthetically, and a prototype is about seeing to it the product functions conceptually. An MVP stays online, functioning, and generating business.

Lesson 6: Co-location is essential.

Although we had modern telecommuting technologies, developing alongside designers made exponential distinction underway. In the corporate environment where it is so simple to get drawn right into other conferences and various other projects, being co-located guarantees working with the exact same things. It included twice the quantity of time to do each experiment.

Lesson 7: Use "pivot or stand firm" efficiently.

We had a hard time obtaining on-line website traffic, which led us to develop an in-store booth, considering that foot website traffic was already involving buy that product. Our emphasis shifted to an end to finish test hereafter pivot, which started guiding our instructions. As opposed to focusing on online business, which was the initial worth recommendation, we rotated to an in-store experience. We started testing modern technology security rather than customer actions. We knew ramifications of our pivot and wished that as soon as the technology works, we can obtain users to place orders without a snag.

Lesson 8: Team members are service companions, and exec is the capitalist.

It took us time to lose our titles and roles and started assuming like business owners. I helped with product cataloguing, setting up stand out files, planning, taking care of, and shaping the organization. Programmers and product managers obtained comfy performing use tests. I got comfortable with various other employees making eleventh-hour UX modifications, and I recognized the tests would certainly show ramifications, and we can repeat. Way of thinking was extremely various; the borders of duties became fuzzy.

Lesson 9: Respect enterprise boundaries.

Regardless of our team is an outlier, there were points we could not ignore; safety and security, lawful, outside vendors, and brand name photos are few of those things. Simple points like sending out advertising e-mails or capturing consumer information on our scrappy site was a worry since dealing with such data is sensitive. Assistance teams fit our ad-hoc demand and prolonged an assisting hand once they comprehended how we got on a start-up journey. Outside suppliers attempted their best to offer solutions to make sure that we didn't reduce. Conflicting top priorities emerged regularly and impacted our cadence, but important service on other jobs couldn't be disregarded.

Build-measure-learn is an excellent procedure for start-ups, and they have nothing to shed, yet an enterprise has existing service and clients that trust this brand and stakes are greater. Several of my most significant style difficulties were around exactly how to offer designs at regular UX team meetings. Every other project was going through the normal review and approval process, but I was approving my own choices. Feedback flowed in these meetings; however, it was testing to include the UX team's comments since the hypotheses for the upcoming sprints were various. The style group injected their suggestions based upon their experience or what they have carried out in the past or pointing out incongruities with design patterns. The style was off a lot of times because designers made a concession to construct that feature quickly and cheap to get it out and examine it. The design was progressing; however, that was an agonizing process for the rest of the team.

Lesson 10: Specify an end to the Lean Start-up process.

The number one question we obtained was when our lean phase will certainly end. Most of us recognized that at some point, we need to leave testing and incorporate our service with the primary e-commerce platform. We didn't have a response in our situation, and we stated it would end when we know that we have stopped working or prospered. Lean start-up enabled us to be creative while making feasible services.

All team members were equipped to form and affect an item's result equally. The team understood when they were jeopardizing the end-user experience. The team understood exactly how to experience style was the glue that attached different parts of item and technology to customers, and I understood how service and metrics could be enjoyable. Lean start-up is a terrific choice for screening unclear item concepts, permitting these suggestions to develop can cause outstanding insights. It's an enjoyable and revitalizing trip that I recommend for any enterprise task.

THE LEAN START-UP: ADVANTAGES AND DIS-MERIT

Searching for a viable service design

Considered that you are in research mode, it is necessary to accept some easy procedures to make sure the search for a scalable company model is a reliable one. In numerous means, these are lessons in active-- efficiency, where time and money are priceless, and the basis for informed decision making is mostly on the back of developing what they call a Minimum Viable Product (MVP). An MVP is a standard version of the item that can be sent out to some clients (ideally early adopters) who will offer you feedback, which will assist you in determining what to do following.

In effect, Ries is recommending that you look for 'proof of demand' prior to constructing the total product, and a very easy way to evaluate for this is to observe real user behaviour, on say, a website. Every click on a button signals intent, no matter whether the product in the back end is there or otherwise, and this information helps you assess likely to need.

Extra Lean Start-up Concepts

The following stands for a short description of several of the major principles connected with the Lean start-up strategy.

1. Examination Often and Find Out Rapidly

As the above example of the MVP, the method showed, they recommend that you don't construct an elaborate product before you have actually taken on many examinations along the way.

2. Observe and Gauge Real Client Behaviour

Eschew focus groups and view exactly how genuine clients act. Obtaining the MVP right into the hands of real clients early on and rapidly gaining from what they do underpins their entire approach.

3. Emphasis Exclusively on Capturing Actionable Metrics

Prevent vanity metrics i.e., metrics that produce a good impact regarding performance when they are illusory. For example: what good is 1 million web page impacts if none of them convert? Rather business owners require to focus on workable metrics i.e., actual metrics that can inform choices.

4. Be Comfortable Pivoting based on Secret Learnings

The recommend you pivot or quit what you are doing if the initial plan is not working (and your searching for support the view that transforming tack is more likely to be successful than continuing with the initial plan).

5. Embrace New Accountancy Techniques

Generally Accepted Accounting Principles (GAAP) has underpinned economic accounting for several years. Nevertheless, Ries argues that Lean Start-ups require to accept 'development bookkeeping' prior to they get to the point where standard bookkeeping kicks in. With this technique, he suggests that development is best tracked by observing things like the individual task, interaction, retention, and vitality. Simply put, if individual numbers are increasing, and they are being maintained such that Life Time worth (LTV) is expanding significantly, this is a far better indication of 'progress' than conventional accountancy techniques.

6. Remain Lean

The word 'lean' describes speed and dexterity and not 'cost savings' as some visitors misunderstand (although that claim, they are against waste 'of all roles'). Again, Ries is recommending that start-ups capitalize on the exploration setting to rapidly learn what is not working so they can make changes quickly.

Some Criticism

Like all 'new principles,' the strategy has its reasonable share of movie critics also. Some individuals cite the lack of effective backers as troublesome, and others concentrate on Ries' reasonably underwhelming profession before writing a guide. For me, I really feel that despite the idea, people will certainly constantly locate flaws and have solid counterarguments to specific components of the method.

THE LIMITS OF THE LEAN START-UP APPROACH

Advocates of the lean start-up technique for creating a business advice business owner, in addition to corporate entrepreneurs, to record, examine, and improve their assumptions concerning a brand-new venture's company model using client discussions and experiments. In general, the lean start-up technique works. We measured success by looking at just how groups carried out in a pitch competition in front of a panel of market experts at the end of the accelerator program (a proxy, albeit an incomplete one, for lasting monetary performance).

Teams that elucidated and afterward tested theories concerning their venture carried out virtually three times much better in the pitch competition more than those teams that did not evaluate any kind of hypotheses. There was no actual, relationship between the number of verified hypotheses and a team's succeeding success. In short, more recognition is not better. I also located that groups that conducted both flexible discussions and more defined try-outs customers in fact done worse in the competitors than teams that conducted either one or the other during the onset of endeavour layout. One possible description for the reduction and also adverse return on consumer interaction is a disintegration of self-confidence:

Excessive comments from customers may trigger the business owners to transform the idea so frequently that they come to be disheartened.

Another possibility is that the lean start-up method, while reliable contrasted to the conventional strategy of "construct it and they will come," still calls for time, focus, and sources that are diverted from various other projects. At some point, managers lack perseverance for continued screening and disengage. Some suggestions should have to die fast and passing if they do not produce consumer demand. The lean start-up approach may be producing "false negatives," meaning good concepts are incorrectly turned down due to the fact that the strategy does not have a clear policy for when entrepreneurs and entrepreneurs ought to state victory, stop testing, and start scaling production. On top of that, business owners should ask themselves which elements of the business design they ought to think about first. Are all aspects of a company model equally crucial in the early design phase?

In my research with clean tech business owners, I found that groups that focused their screening on the triumvirate of target customer sector, value recommendation, and network performed twice in addition to teams that did not spend much interest on those three categories. The popularity of the lean start-up method is well should have. True of any company procedure, the approach should be customized and used with representation and constraints, not blind allegiance. Much like the new ventures it creates, it will certainly boost as researchers and professionals suggest, examination, and integrate improvements.

LEAN ANALYTICS

"Everyone believes they have the best vision for their product, which they recognize their individuals. However, the fact is they do not." Those may seem like rough words. In his function as Vice Head of state of Item at Amplitude, Justin Bauer has experienced business firms spend many hours and countless dollars to launch, not successful products. According to Justin, bigger businesses commonly fall short of developing the right remedies since their apparently bottomless sources can be disadvantageous. For example, a huge spending plan can stop a team from making thoughtful decisions and bring about nothing more than lost money. How exactly do you prevent your business from investing in the incorrect concept? To locate the solution, we recently did a partner webcast with Justin, and we have actually put together some of his best pointers for making use of item analytics to inspire beneficial and speedy development.

Begin with the data

In Justin's experience, without data, groups entrusted with constructing a new item usually base choices on office national politics, suggesting either the most senior or highest possible paid individual in the room will certainly determine the result.

"Basically, that individual begins this waterfall process where the firm will certainly construct something that isn't useful to the customer since they really did not have the ideal understanding of what the client wants, and it wastes months, if not years, to arrive," he says. The very first step to making certain that corporate culture does not weaken the procedure is to collect data. Justin advises first checking out the numbers to recognize the problem you're considering solving and then releasing something promptly to determine the influence. A tiny success can be the start of continual dedication to data-driven learning.

Justin encourages, "Discover that win that then you can use to persuade the rest of the organization, "This need to be something we must buy." From there, I believe you can develop a possible company situation as to why you need something like an item analytic solution such that the whole company can do [the same thing]".

Find your magic number

Taking a look at any and every item of data will certainly not prove useful, however. "In the end, what I recommend is one [number] Figure out what statistics associates with your [desired] service outcome," Justin suggests. "The truth is, I can't inform you what that metric will be for your company. It, in fact, truly depends on your clients."

Below are a few actions Justin recommends for locating your most important metric.

1. Determine your vital events According to Justin, those are tasks that deliver value to your consumers.

"Instances of crucial occasions for our clients might be things like completing a purchase, adding us onto a checklist, or running a question," he says.

2. Understand exactly how essential events affect business outcomes, such as earnings or engagement.

3. Track the vital occasion that the majority of favourable influences wanted company end results.

4. End up being obsessed with your consumers (in a healthy means).

Once you can determine your service against critical occasions, you can (and should) end up being client stressed, Justin says. Do whatever you can to comprehend exactly how brand-new products and features influence clients, with the objective of only building points that enhance preferred results. As an example, if you release a new product attribute, ask: What percentage of your individuals are really making use of the new feature, and how did that number affect your best service result?

One more essential action is decentralizing decision-making and zeroing in on customer problems, not demands. Justin claims having individuals who are close to the client choose is "actually, really important." This also makes certain that the item group is linked to your customers." [The item group] cannot be outsourcing that to the analytics division since then [item] cycles are most likely to take weeks prior to they reach the following degree understanding, and that simply remains to slow them down.

Establish a 10X vision.
Provide a 10% model

As the data gathers and your consumers disclose a laundry list of problems, your company will certainly think up big services. This is what Justin calls 10X vision. You need to comprehend what are the core issues that you wish to resolve for, but after that, a great deal of times individuals will attempt to construct this enormous product to strike that vision. It takes a year for it to go out. We claim, "No, think about the 10 percent thing that you might develop to validate it if that is the appropriate vision."

Lean start-up and Lean Analytics in the Venture

In my study, I talked with a lot of entrepreneurs working at a selection of various firms (innovation, telecommunications, media, publishing, etc.) and came away with some fascinating and somewhat (in my mind), unusual understandings. I intended to share those with you like the discussion around Lean Start-up, and Lean Analytics continues to broaden.

1. It's currently happening

Granted, there's prejudice here due to the fact that I spoke especially with people that have applied Lean techniques in their companies, but I was amazed at how considerable their work has been. It was motivating to realize that people are implementing Lean and obtaining results; they just don't share publicly similarly that start-ups do.

2. JFDI

I asked every person I talked with concerning exactly how they obtained the Lean methodology into their company. The answer was easy, "We simply did it." Someone (when he has designated a brand-new project) started it off by informing people they'd go talk to customers first, before constructing something. Every person around the table just presumed that's just how points functioned, so they followed along. And voila, Lean had infiltrated the company. There's a chance to be stealthy/sneaky concerning using Lean: begin small and simply do it. Individuals will certainly adhere to along.

3. Presentation matters

Information individuals have not a problem checking out and sorting through great deals of information. Every person requires things provided in basic and consistent means. You need to make scorecards and focus on vital metrics that will really resonate. Even if supervisors request "a lot more information," they do not truly wish to see even more information. They desire answers to inquiries. And consistency is vital-- you require to reveal the same point over and over and over again for people to comprehend its relevance.

4. The metrics are changing

It's happening gradually. I most definitely see a fad (particularly in consulting with posting and media companies) in the direction of workable metrics. Web page views will always be a thing, and now the focus gets on funnels and user engagement. And they're simplifying as well. In a few cases, people had complete individual habits lifecycle mapped out, and then they were piercing right into particular areas, running brief experiments, and trying to boost those things.

5. Do not call it Lean Start-up

This isn't something I considered, but it turned up a few times. People are devouring Lean Start-up (the book), and other material, but when they bring the ideas right into their organizations, they do not call it "Lean Start-up." Similar to my initial point over, they simply bring it in as a brand-new way of doing things. The word "start-up" appears to terrify people in larger companies; they do not assume it'll apply to them. A few people informed me that their bosses/managers don't think such as the idea of espousing or being married to any type of one approach or approach. If you're seeking to bring Lean into your business, go down the "Start- up" and just concentrate on the actual to- dos and finest methods.

6. Getting all the information you require is hard

Huge organizations have things all over the place. It's not always clear what is what and gradually data gets stuck in disparate systems handled by diverse teams. One person I talked to informed me that she spent six months just finding out where everything was and piecing together what they had. Just at that point was she able to determine what data factors they were missing out on and begin collecting those. It's a huge endeavour to attempt and combine different information silos, but it's an essential step to developing a solid structure.

7. Evaluate brand-new item concepts and turn them right into functions

New products that you evaluate swiftly as experiments (against an existing user base-- which big firms generally have) may not become new products that you launch. You might find functions that can be integrated right into existing products. They'll build tiny mobile apps (or sites) on the side, testing against certain metrics (typically engagement associated) and see what occurs. They do not wind up with a totally new product, but they've discovered a feature that functions well for their existing product. We usually see start-ups identified as "features, not items"-- which for start-ups is a negative thing. For entrepreneurs, it might not be, since they can roll those features into an existing product, and they've already proven the advantages (albeit on a smaller sized scale, in a speculative method). This type of innovation is remarkable.

How to Utilize Lean Analytics in Mobile Video Game Growth

Lean Start-up is Data-Driven

Aviv began working for Lot of money 100 business in a corporate atmosphere in information when data analytics was called "service knowledge," he claimed. No matter what you call it, Aviv stated the objective of analytics is locating a means to utilize information to benefit a service. Aviv applauded the Lean Start-up method for being intrinsically data-driven, a good marketing factor when you're attempting to convince creators or a little item group to invest in information analytics. "Each of the stages, like build, determine, discover, has integrated right into it [a] data-intrinsic method," Aviv mentioned.

Convincing product development groups to do A/B screening beforehand-- in which you produced two versions of a product and services and see which variation is far better-- can be a difficult fight, Aviv said, so Lean Start-up is a terrific method to take. Aviv pertained to Lean Start-up after what he called a normal start-up experience, "the falling short kind" that was likewise instructional. After bootstrapping an information scientific research application for about a year that "we made sure was going to alter the world" just to have it fail, it led Aviv to ask how they were developing remedies.

Ask the Right Questions

The business he advises currently, Social Factor, is well developed in the gaming market and has a strong customer base, yet it still deals with the exact same difficulties of how to obtain and use the information it looks for. Aviv claimed prior to they even create a new video game they start by asking, "What is a great game?"

Then they determine which indicators will certainly help them confirm the product-market fit of the first version of a brand-new video game. Aviv makes use of Lean Start-up to recognize the ideal inquiries to ask that will certainly create data solutions. "Within Lean Start-up, you find out there are entrances, depending upon the stage of the product, you understand which KPIs (crucial efficiency indicators) you need to focus on, and which metrics matter most." For every single new video game, they try to launch two or even more versions of the video game. "One that's, claim, manage untouched, and one with the renovations you wish to gauge," Aviv said.

Confirm Prior To Evaluating

When asked exactly how Social Factor verifies a suggestion for a video game before a product even exists, Aviv explained a method of play screening, a form of qualitative evaluation, in which the video game is presented in 2 ways to 2 target markets. The very first variation of the game may be a bit more than a mock-up of display shots aimed at a target market that is familiar with video games, such as creators of other pc gaming business. The 2nd version may be a low-tech model focused on a target market that is consisted of gamers knowledgeable about these kinds of video games.

Several of these prototypes are done with really minimal investment, Aviv clarified, and usually really little coding. If it has to do with a much more complex technological remedy, we generally just use screenshots and explain the concept of it." After test users have actually tried them out, Aviv said they talk to their users and verify suggestions with them. "Anything that does not include, as we state in the Lean Start-up technique, leaving the structure [or] engaging with the genuine market will certainly always be prejudiced. Yet it can offer you some extremely valuable hints and guidelines regarding ... what appeals to people [or] what is not very efficient."

Try To Find Actionable Metrics

Just because a company catches data, does not suggest that data remains in and of itself valuable or workable. Some metrics are just vanity metrics. "If you can inform me within a particular market that gadgets of a specific rate are a lot more interesting, that's something I can work with. I can transform the means I target," Aviv clarified.

Lean Analytics, Aviv stated, help "differentiate and differentiate" between the metrics that are not useful and the ones that are. For instance, if he's checking out two metrics, conversion, or average investment, the conversion is a lot more difficult and would need more screening, so ordinary spend is going to be one of the most workable. "The decision regarding what am I going to be determining at which stage of the game has very remarkable effects on what I am creating, which features of the video game I'm concentrating my focus on," Aviv said.

Anticipate Positive and Negative Influences

Simply presenting a brand-new function is no assurance of getting favourable comments from customers, Aviv warned. Sometimes a brand-new feature in a video game will certainly be a hit with a small subset of individuals and have an extremely unfavourable response on others. It is necessary to recognize user accounts in advance. However, even adverse feedback is important in shaping how they turn out brand-new functions.

"The best scientific means to evaluate [a brand-new] feature is to launch a variation just with that said, wait, launch an additional version," Aviv claimed.

This does slow down the advancement procedure. However, that might be the most effective way to track down which of the changes are the most reliable with the customer base. If the input is originating from a small sample of individuals, Aviv suggested taking it with a grain of salt, yet if a larger example of customers is providing negative responses, then that data is most likely actionable. "You actually require to comprehend your users and have the ability to pay attention to them," Aviv insisted. "Try versions, see what occurs, and see what works."

Integrate Tracking

Figuring out which tools a firm needs for data collection can be a process of screening in and of itself. Nonetheless, Aviv advised integrating tracking right into products. When a person downloads a game, Social Factor tracks such things as when someone purchases, when a person logs into the video game, and when someone clicks a battle. Every one of these should be thought about in product growth. "That's pieces of code you integrate, and sensing units you take into your game to be able to see what individuals are taking pleasure in, what they're playing," Aviv claimed. This can slow down advancement, so he advised attempting to do this "without breaking the speed of the product. You need to be very lean regarding how you approach analytics."

The secret is to concentrate on a really little collection of metrics that are workable. "Don't try to cover whatever, do not try to track whatever."

Lean Start-up and Lean Analytics remains in the Business

There's a lot of jobs still to do. We need more individuals coming forward and sharing their stories. It's clear that Lean Start-up and Lean Analytics are firmly growing themselves in the enterprise and making a difference. Entrepreneurs aren't asking for consent, and they're simply moving forward and doing it. The company guidelines still apply-- you need air cover, you require financial support, etc. but things are relocating. It was interesting and motivating to talk with entrepreneurs at large multinationals and realize that they're, in many cases, even more, active and nimble than numerous start-ups I have actually talked with. When they get to applying Lean and running experiments, they have actually got substantial resources (user base, web website traffic, bucks, and so on) to put to good use.

How to Use Lean Principles to Your Start-up's Performance

Applying "lean" to productivity in start-ups

Today, lean principles have been put on nearly every market, both large and small scale. For instance, lean principles in the health care sector have actually had the ability to lower costs while boosting effectiveness. On a smaller sized scale, staff members have actually used these concepts to organize their workspaces. Right here are four ways you can use lean concepts to your start- up to boost both performance and high quality.

Boost your work environment using the five principles of lean

Value: Value suggests placing yourself in your consumer's footwear and understanding what their requirements are. This helps you determine timelines, rates and expectations as opposed to constant experimentation. For your group, letting them recognize exactly how they fit into the bigger picture can keep them inspired.

Value stream: Worth stream is where you create a "value stream" of all the actions and procedures required in getting the end product or solution to your clients. This could consist of design, manufacturing, shipment, Human Resources and customer care. Understanding this info enables you to get rid of any kind of wasteful steps.

Flow: After you've removed any kind of unnecessary waste from the value stream, you wish to see to it that everything runs smoothly. Circulation indicates not having any disruptions or hold-ups. The circulation entails breaking down steps, levelling out work, developing cross-functional departments, and training your team so they can create multiple abilities.

Draw: When flow enhances, so does the moment it requires to obtain your goods or solutions to consumers. Due to this, they can "pull" whenever needed, so you're not continuously under- or overproducing stock, material, etc.

Perfection: Even after effectively completing the first steps, you still require to continuously keep working to enhance procedures to make sure that you can eliminate waste. Perfection might be a lofty objective in whatever endeavour we are pursuing-- yet we still must constantly be progressing towards being the very best and attaining the most effective.

Make use of the idea of 5S to get yourself arranged. 5S stands for kind, ordered, shine, systematize and endure.

You can use this principle to arrange your office, so you and your team are a lot more productive by doing the following:

- Remove any type of item that you no longer need (sort).
- Organize your continuing to be things, so you're much more

efficient (align).

- Keep your work area spick-and-span, so you can locate items and recognize troubles quicker (sparkle).

- Colour-code and tag files and schedules to make you much more regular (systematize).

- Establish repeatable habits and habits that will certainly maintain your office clean and arranged, such as completing one job prior to moving onto the next (maintain).

You and your team-- even if they're virtual employees working from an office-- can start by throwing out anything unwanted. Place files right into closets-- color-coded your schedules-- and keep things you often utilize close by. These principles aren't just restricted to physical items. Electronically, you can use a task administration system to designate tasks, rapidly see the development of tasks, and share documents and remarks in one arranged dashboard. Systematize your work to come to be more reliable.

In production, there's a conventional procedure for every little thing. The reason? By doing something the same way time and time again, you will get rid of a waste considering that you're not continuously experimenting with new strategies. Systematizing also prevents errors and forgetfulness because there's a checklist forever before the action of the trip. For instance, when a car gets on the production line, it cannot progress if a person neglected a screw or set up a faulty steering wheel.

Standardize what makes sense

Start by maintaining a time log to see when you're most efficient and exactly how you're spending your time. You may observe that you're most efficient in the mornings. If so, that's when you need to deal with your most important task. If you uncover that you're checking your email and social accounts frequently, routine specific times throughout the day to inspect them, to prevent wasteful conferences, you can standardize conferences. Make certain these meetings are needed and include just key individuals pertinent to the information. Maintain all meetings as brief and succinct as feasible. Get involved in a good flow to maximize your and your group's performance. Flow is merely just how a job can progress through use of a system. When your system is running smoothly, circulation is excellent. When flow strikes a snag, it slows down the procedure, and waste happens.

Manufacturing centres make it a point to make certain that the flow is great. Unless it's an emergency situation, production lines hardly ever quit running. Everyone has a specific task to do, and that's all they're focused on. That's not the instance at your start-up. You should put on numerous hats, as well as manage continuous disturbances. The number of times have you been in "the area" and obtained side tracked by a telephone call or have no choice however, to go produced a fire?

Remember emphasis

One way you can enhance circulation in your start-up is by concentrating on something each time. That means say goodbye to multitasking. Offer your 100 percent emphasis on what you're working on currently and then proceed to your next job. This may take some self- discipline. However, you can begin by switching off all press alerts, shutting your door, block scheduling and establishing borders. You can assist your group to boost their flow by establishing "do not interrupt" areas and time frames.

THE MIT BLACKJACK GROUP: AN EFFICIENT START-UP MODEL

Starting a business is no tiny or easy task. Hundreds of hours enter into making plans and contingencies for those strategies. Every one of this prep work steps usually heads out the window as quickly as you make your very first advertising telephone call. Entrepreneurs are constantly searching for that magic book or article that will catapult their organization to the top tiers of success. I'm positive that no such fool proof text exists. Like all points in service, there are exceptions to policies. The exceptions in these circumstances come in the kind of nuggets of wisdom supplied by overtly successful business individuals.

Cards for gain and loss

For those that don't understand, Ed Thorp is most likely the most effective straight cash manager in the background. The unofficial billionaire is the Godfather of card checking-- the first approach used to turn around engineer online casino games for profit. This method seeded the concept of the MIT Blackjack Team in the very early 1990s.The MIT groups were managed and moneyed by two males that used the student body of MIT as a labour force to discover possible skilled card counters. Seems rather simple right? Not so much. But what these two founders had that varies from a typical start-up was that their cost was basically absolutely no.

Tapping the hive for employee bees

Often times business throws away hundreds of dollars, educating an individual to do a barely appropriate job. Not here. The success of the person leads to success for the organization.

This principle typically avoids most brand-new companies. An effective facet of the MIT Blackjack Team start-up model is that the worker comes with no cost to the organization. A firm's profits driving concepts are frequently defined in extremely broad terms; the information is not important to the basic labour force. The nature of an MIT pupil, especially in the STEM programs where most of the MIT gamers were touched, is inquisitiveness. Wish can just take a prospect up until now. They have to use the gained expertise of the system. Initially, they use it in the manner in which has no economic repercussions, after that, in a way that has only minimal economic consequences. After that, when players are skilled in implementing specific income creating techniques, they can transfer to levels where the profit margins have the capacity for extraordinary making power.

Moving from genuine money to digital money

Once they're experienced in the system, they can proceed to genuine money video gaming. Prior to prominent Web gambling, this needed going to a gambling enterprise and playing for reduced risks. Now gamers can simply log-on to a web site and examine their abilities. For example, 888 Casino is an on the internet gambling establishment that has actual suppliers that deal with every significant casino site video game in real-time. Roulette, Craps, and Blackjack, are all there for gamers to play. This genuine dealership application gives the player a preference of what live play resembles. This testing phase needs to be customized to a start-up's market, yet the generalized principle stands for all entrepreneurs. If the company is a finance fund, a digital profile can be developed to check the techniques to back-test and validate that the method got on the right side of market activities. For management, this is a procedure for providing an individual an increasing number of power and obligation, when their choices are verified to be audio.

Using the lessons

The crucial point approaches, demonstrated by the development of the MIT teams are, first, pick your workers from a large and extremely gifted group of individuals. Below the best of the best rise to the top and the talent swimming pool is self-regulating. Next, show your staff members where the approach you will utilize comes from and allow them to create their abilities. Give them chances to ensure that they can display their proficiency for an offered task. What makes these methods so reliable is that there is no charge to developing skills in the company. There is no chance cost associated with the learning curve in an organization. By negating the talent advancement price, a firm can spend money on the earnings producing elements of the organization.

Hostility over Passivity

By finding out the standard strategy for blackjack, gamers can considerably lower the gambling establishment's advantage from 3% down to 0.5% for every single hand. Though players can discover this technique, theoretically, many of them still struggle to make the right choice when playing at gambling enterprise floors or on-line blackjack. The natural propensity is for the player to stand pat on this hand (not take a card) in the hopes that the dealer himself will have to take a card and will breast."

Statistics show how this easy approach, as a matter of fact, triggers a lot more problems for the player in the future and is the main reason numerous players fall short of winning. Instead of staying with the basic strategy and being the assailant, the gamers that select to be passive location power into the hands of the dealer, which undoubtedly results in their failure. From an entrepreneur's viewpoint, this exact same logic can be applied. Success in business never ever originated from being passive, and leaders must be prepared to make challenging choices for the good of the firm instead of avoiding them. Hesitation and question will undoubtedly lead to failure, and an entrepreneur should be strong-minded, figured out, and absolutely confident of what needs to be done.

Knowledge Is Power

Understanding every facet of the video game is most importantly important when carrying out the basic method in blackjack. Card-counters depend on information to make those winning choices, and they need to stick to the protocol and set plan whatsoever times in spite of whether their impulses are telling them otherwise. With this in mind, an entrepreneur's most reliable device when building their service is expertise. By learning everything they can regarding the marketplace they are associated with, concerning their competitors, about their client, about their item, and regarding the history of the sector they are operating in, they can utilize that knowledge to make crucial choices that drive the firm onward.

Failure is a Necessary Evil

When the stakes are high at the blackjack table, a loss can seem disastrous, and also the best card-counters in the world have experienced them at some point in their occupations. Suffice to say, Ma's accomplishments in blackjack and various other locations of his life have much surpassed his failures, and this component of self-belief and belief in one's technique is something entrepreneurs need to aspire to.

HOW TO USE LEAN PRINCIPLES TO TIME MANAGEMENT

Lean administration is a relevant philosophy that can boost manufacturing whatsoever levels of an organization. Continual improvement should be your criterion for your own work as well as that of employees. Lean principles not just boost productivity, yet also allow leaders to understand exactly how workers react to Lean changes. Empowerment and liability begin on the first stage; however, they have to not stop there.

3 Lean Principles for Time Administration

Right here are three methods of Lean assuming you can use today to far better handle your time.

Maintain the "Consumer" In Mind

When you do not "believe Lean," you will likely begin your day with the job that presents itself first. Rather, make a routine of taking 10 minutes every morning, without diversions, to prioritize your work based on its worth to the many "clients" you offer.

What will stakeholder's most worth from you today?

This kind of thinking may lead you to discover that you are investing the lion's share of your performance on jobs that are not valued by key "clients."

Use Worth Stream Mapping

Value stream mapping is utilized to chart an item's trip from resources to the end individual, with the goal of eliminating waste. You can make use of approximately the very same strategy to a lot more effectively manage tasks that need your engagement, but also for which you are not solely accountable. Let us state that your firm is preparing a public statement regarding an item recall in your sector. The "basic materials"-- an outline-- will be sourced from a communications manager. The declaration than "circulations" up the chain to you for authorization, potentially traveling through multiple communicators and your lawful team in the process.

When you have actually weighed in, the draft will certainly recede to your communications team and be delivered by a firm leader. If you dedicate five minutes to sketching a time administration worth stream map prior to appointing this kind of work, you might locate that your original plan would compel you to wait for redundant responses, or would delay the declaration's release by delivering it to you for editing and enhancing at a troublesome time. By comprehending the circulation of this "item," you can guarantee that it is provided more effectively.

Look out for Wasteful Injury

Decrease of unnecessary activity is a common Lean management goal, usually targeting production line staff members. Along similar lines, you might be losing efficient time since your functioning style creates unnecessary discomfort, causing pause and/or constant breaks during the day. Take into consideration having your workstation examined by a comfort design professional. As opposed to waiting until your level of productivity has actually been reduced by pain to stretch, timetable short breaks to walk around your office, and limber up. When possible, make use of a flexible work desk to alternate between standing and sitting.

15 Tips To a Much More Efficient and Better Lean Start-up Team

To remain competitive, a company must discover methods to inspire its crucial brand name ambassadors-- the employees. In as much as customers are necessary, a staff base that is bastardized and dulled presents an upcoming disaster in the business. It is important to keep your workers feeling wanted, liked, encouraged, and constantly encouraged every day. Begin with any one of these 15 pointers and execute them by integrating this right into your business society. These tips will certainly demonstrate how to transform your staff members from standard and dull to excited ambassadors of your brand name, thus enhancing their efficiency.

1. Budget for books/Library

Books are not very costly. The various other good side is that books can constantly be shared. Completion outcome is that you create a culture of reading in your employees. Individuals that learn more learn more. You desire your staff members to never quit learning. This boosts their database and productivity. When you have actually bought a lot of publications, you will have a collection where your group can obtain whatever publication they have not to check out if they require to cool off or just have a brand-new experience. By motivating employees to produce analysis checklists and share them with each other, your business's reading society strengthens. New employees can be cultivated into this society once they enter the business. More publications only make your workers better and brighter.

2. Stockpile on beer and hard liquor

Functioning while intoxicated is not something any person should encourage in their business. Even those that consumers don't intend to do it throughout the working days or while in the office. Stock up your business's beer rack and give some hard liquor due to the fact that your employees won't drink at work anyways. What's the point? It's for them to recognize that the start-up firm they help is totally free and autonomous. When they know they are enabled to consume at the workplace, it improves their spirits since, especially when they have a rough day, they can just get hold of one container of beer, often even after the job.

3. Workshops & webinars

Workshops benefit your staff members, as are webinars. This could be a little expensive, particularly when they need to travel much for the workshops. However, they acquire a lot of expertise from these workshops. Teaming up with your human resource department guarantees that the staff members apply what they discover to accomplish the firm's objectives. The concept of being outside the work environment for a workshop likewise delights a lot of workers.

4. Work environment re-modelling

Any easy method to do your office transformation when you have money is to update the furniture that your staff members utilize or do a redesign of your office right into a better working place. Stats reveal that enhancing your workplace's design alone raises staff member efficiency by 17%. When your start-up isn't on a huge budget plan, enabling your employees to customize their job work desks will certainly increase their performance by 32%. This enables them to put pictures of their enjoyed ones on their work desks and installed a wall surface packed with tasks to complete or even carry their most favoured art sculpture to their work desks in the workplace. Various other start-ups have a 'Pimp My Desk' Day, where employees complete for a present card on who has pimped their desk better Do It

Yourself design in as much as that could be very loved one.

5. Develop a Fun and Creative Workplace

You could develop innovative office space for your staff members, especially if it's suggested to be an open strategy office. Rather than lumping your workers together outdoors strategy office, discover creative developers who will make an open strategy workplace that promotes your employees for the better. Add some enjoyable into your office by having a dartboard, for instance, or blackboard, where people write their concepts or go to brainstorm when they are tired from remaining on their computer systems throughout the day.

6. Reward campaign

Founders begin firms giving the core product, and while that is a huge success, the most successful companies today really did not depend on that one idea from the founder to endure. As the creator, you need to urge creative thinking in the business. You should likewise value that you are dealing with creative individuals. This leads us to the following factor. Given that they are creative people, they will think of several suggestions to boost the core product. Pay attention to these ideas. The most effective companies in the world today are built on the foundation of paying attention to workers. Compensate the best suggestions and incorporate them into the core item to see exactly how they influence the firm's primary service. Do not trash concepts that originate from your team; even when they might not be the best concepts, award the staff member anyways for taking the initiative.

7. A Getaway Recreation room

As your firm continues to grow, you can integrate a video gaming room in your office for employees as a vacation. Incorporating video games like table-tennis in there can provide staff members something to unwind their minds when they require to. Make certain to develop tufted wall surfaces as acoustic shields that protect against the sound from the recreation room from spilling into the rest of the workplace where a great deal of concentration is continuous. A video PC gaming centre can be incorporated specifically if the majority of your workers are programmers and designers. These are the kind that plays a lot of computer game and may take advantage of a 30 minute break in your pc gaming areas.

8. Offer choices for sitting

From bag chairs to faces and standing workstations, there is a range of seats you can offer in your business. Don't do the fundamental "workplace chair with lumbar assistance" thing. Be various. Most workers don't like the standard business seats anyway. By supplying those conventional workplace chairs while spicing them up with bag chairs and standing workstations, your present choices to staff members who have been resting on one seat for a long period of time.

9. Clear interaction

Communication is a vital part of anything. From businesses to families and relationships, clear interaction can make or damage you. A start-up is no various. Make certain to clearly interact with your business's objectives to your group and provide time to process these and ask inquiries. Provide them with at least 3 hrs. to process the info and return with questions if they might have any type of. Clear interaction enhances a workplace and makes sure things run efficiently, producing a great deal for everyone.

10. Purchase Training

Having flexible staff members enhances the total performance of the firm—this result must not translate right into a "Jack of All Trades" scenario. Investing in training your staff members in abilities they are bad at will make them far better individuals in general. For example, when you have programmers in your firm, they might not be as great in using applications like MS Excel or PowerPoint. For a couple of dollars, on-line training platforms like Demy or Coursera could be really valuable here. Somewhere along the line our programmers know just how to organize the information correctly utilizing Excel before they present it to you, making use of MS PowerPoint. When workers see you investing in their knowledge of side abilities that boost their core ability, it provides much more motivation to create much better results for the company.

11. Smart Delegation of Tasks

Delegation of jobs can get jobs finished, yet if done wrong, it will certainly cause bastardized or strained employees. Smart delegation involves studying your employees toughness and weak points before designating tasks to them. This ensures that each worker obtains the tasks in fields they are really proficient at. That's a balanced circumstance. The wrong circumstance would certainly be where one of the most dedicated staff members are provided all tasks to finish while various other staff members have a lot more leisure time or obtain a great deal fewer tasks to complete. Completion outcome is hardworking staff members who are tired out and various other staff members that really feel bastardized because they are underutilized.

12. Team Building activities

Group building results in the development of individual bonds between workers. The team reaches find out more regarding each other. These tasks don't always have to be outside, even though outdoor occasions are a lot more encouraged or favoured when your spending plan enables that. You can have team building indoor occasions where you take time off the workplace work to play video games or share drinks and stuff like that. This fosters better partnerships at the office, shares like, and causes happier workers whose spirits run out of the roof covering.

13. Have Smaller Groups

Smaller teams have actually proven to be the most effective groups. Jeff Bezos, Amazon's Chief Executive Officer, preserves that if a team cannot be fed by two pizzas, it's also big. The study has actually also proved that in larger groups, people feel less responsible for anything than in smaller groups. Remember that larger groups are a waste of everybody's time despite the size of the task. Smaller sized groups will result in greater productivity rates and high quality work.

14. Job Monitoring Equipment instead of Meetings

Instead of having countless conferences to inspect where your team has gotten to on their jobs, job management devices like Basecamp and Asana make it feasible for your group to remotely upgrade their progress on various tasks without wasting time with meetings. Research study has actually shown that conferences and teleconference waste 5.6 hrs. of each worker's time every week and reduce total efficiency. People don't choose to be in meetings unless it's essential for them. Innovation and systems like Basecamp have actually made it possible to get rid of that productivity bottleneck.

15. Efficient and Meaningful Responses

The most effective tasks are completed based on productive, truthful and meaningful back-and-forth feedback. This should be your goal when your staff members bring the finished tasks to you for inspecting. Offering purposeful responses to your workers reveals that you are truthful and boosts the general outlook of the administration. It will also create a society of trust fund and personal development, so your team takes pride in boosting their personal performance.

HOW TO ENCOURAGE YOUR WORKERS TO ACT LIKE BUSINESS OWNERS

Educates huge facility organizations and start-ups around the world on how to take on strategic, cultural, and supervisory difficulties by using scientific roughness to the item and business growth. If you're thinking of transforming your firm with an entrepreneurial culture, here are five methods business leaders can encourage employees to imitate business owners.

1. Create Business Disruption

Start-ups obstacle existing service frameworks with new ideas, innovations, and procedures that consumers want. While already recognized companies frequently focus the majority of their power on staying on top of manufacturing demands and activities, entrepreneurs invest their time examining the market to see what brand-new products and services meet an unmet need. For instance, Netflix and Redbox each interfered with the video rental market by providing consumers with very easy accessibility to their favoured motion pictures, with less late fees. By the time Hit and Hollywood Video stepped back from their day-to-day operations to see what took place, it was far too late to conserve their companies. Offer your team authority to do what they believe is right for the consumer and be part of a fully devoted useful team. Trust them with a small amount of financing.

2. Place the Client Front and Facility

Rather than concentrating on what your team can do well, focus on the issue, the consumer is trying to address. This does not imply asking the consumer what they require: instead, beginning by recognizing the customer's organization model and the issue and chance. Lean Start-up groups method techniques like identifying "leap of faith" assumptions, and testing using minimal sensible items. Advancement groups will certainly put models in front of customers that aren't always quiet. Getting this difficult feedback from consumers is just one of the greatest parts of the method, and results in social adjustment. Companies can no more count on traditional marketing research and focus groups if they wish to validate a new option. Clients can inform you of all the viewpoints they want, yet you require to focus on their habits.

3. Invest Resources the Right Way

In order for teams to deal with a start- up frame of mind that enables effective failing (which can be a really terrifying thing), it is essential to create an environment for the leadership group to know what's taking place so that they can be part of the conversation that infuses entrepreneurship right into the culture of the firm. GE has had success with Growth Boards, a team of people that accepts or turns down projects. By putting product groups through a very different funding cycle, GE had the ability to motivate the whole firm to get thrilled concerning a brand-new way of working.

4. Seek Leaders Who Evaluate and Discover

In order to create a culture of discovering and iteration, it is essential to find experts and leaders with the utmost experience who are open to this new way of working. In a world changing at extraordinary rates to keep up with an advancing market, leaders require to be trained to ask the inquiry. "Do you have the humility not to recognize the solution?"? It's far better to have a small team with a greater ability to influence and the courage to claim, "I don't understand, yet allows you go figure it out.

5. Adjustment with The Times

With start-ups nipping at the heels of large corporations, GE has decided that rather than combating the adjustment, they ought to transform with it. With some help from Lean Start-up approaches, they've had the ability to alter the method they function, think, and act day-to-day. They began with 20 projects that Eric aided breed. Individuals, from money to design, enjoyed it. And ultimately, they rolled out this various mind-set. Exactly how? By training executives, producing a brand-new governance framework, making management part of the conversation, and revising business ideas. They created a physical workbook, established an extreme training process and culture change training that plainly laid out the worth's involved in this new means of functioning. The result? They changed individuals' way of thinking and actions.

HANDLING A REMOTE GROUP

It's close, since things are changing right before you, but much of it is because that's where the remote employees are. Not only are even more people functioning from another location, but they are also investing more time away from the workplace. While lots of companies concur, that remote employees tend to be more efficient, the surprising information is how much more. Two-year research recently concluded that remote employees saw an efficiency increase equal to a complete additional day of work.

While belonging to a remote team sounds ingenious and empowering, the reality is handling remote groups to maintain them worked with and on-task can show to be hard. I have the good luck to work with an extremely intense, devoted group that just takes place to be expanded across the earth. The experience   has shown   me   some important lessons on the best techniques for non-local cooperation and understandings right into the future of work. Although remote workers tend to be much more taken part in their work, they need to function harder on the most standard things like interaction. The complying with suggestions have actually assisted our remote team in growing to be much more efficient and well- coordinated:

1. Prepare for Simultaneous Vs. Asynchronous Messaging

Synchronous type of messages somites is referred to channels like phone, video calls, and in-person meetings. Asynchronous consists of email, Slack, message, carrier applications, and anything where you can compose an answer before hitting send out. If your team does not recognize which messages belong in which channel, you will wind up squandering many ways too much time on pointless conference calls, endless email chains, and experiencing notification tiredness. Don't overlook this essential action.

2. Have wonderful thought

This is very closely connected to the point above. Email can be wacky due to the fact that there are no context ideas like tone, inflection, body movement, etc. Individuals tend to interpret messages in a different way depending upon their mood or what they think regarding the writer. Train your team to presume excellent objectives for each message. Due to the fact that my group thinks my favourable regard, I do not need to add faces and exclamation indicate soften the tone of portable messages. This saves us a considerable quantity of time and permits all of us to concentrate on what's actually important.

3. Take care of Expectations

Do this with your team, specifically do this if you deal with suppliers. Ensure your team recognizes with turnaround times, communication methods, and any other constraints or costs related to range. The outmost result is that your team is crystal clear on supplier capabilities and can handle their functional expectations, as necessary.

4. Stay with a consistent path

Consistency in keeping appointments is essential. When you are managing complicated schedules across time zones, a disturbance in the call timetable will create turmoil. Gain consensus on a normal tempo of meeting times and make certain that employee treats this as a top priority. Most remote employees are free spirits who prize self-reliance. It is essential to help them identify that routine conference times are the structure for playing respectfully with others, taking care of uncommon requests for exceptions, and higher efficiency for every person.

5. The video clip

I seem to like this as my crucial tip. We need video calls for every meeting. Conferences must be extracted from a quiet place with high-speed Wi-Fi and ear buds. When team members appear in a specialist method, it suggests fewer diversions and much less time wasted while developing relationships and dealing up efficiency. It lionizes to your customers and fellow employee when you demonstrate that you value their time and give them the specialist courtesy they deserve.

6. Hold Impromptu Video Clip Calls

If you discover an email thread going back and forth greater than three times, relocate away from e-mail. Include the thing to an upcoming program for conversation or hold an unscripted video clip call on Slack. Exercise radical sincerity lives during those telephone calls. Ask sharp inquiries and share actual responses. Employees can't grow unless you test them directly while confirming that you care about them directly. Radical sincerity takes digestive tracts, skill, and compassion, yet it is absolutely needed for handling remote teams. One quick video telephone call can save the entire project.

7. No Agenda. No Fulfilling

My group understands to find ready for every conference-- also everyday stand-ups-- with a program. Pre-select a facilitator and timekeeper and designate a person to document next actions. In remote groups, it's too easy for employees to make presumptions or gloss over vital factors. The end result of recording activities, deadlines, barriers, and ownership is transparency and accountability.

8. Clarifying "Why" Goes a Long Way

The hardest part concerning remote work is feeling neglected and failed to remember. Remote employees frequently lose out on the events that led up to a certain decision or technique. As their supervisor, I now make it a vital part of my process to make sure that they understand the "why" of what I'm asking of them. I take a step back prior to responding or guiding and align the staff member to the goal. This has aided a lot of more delicate employees to comprehend the business situation for asking a concern or elevating a flag and stops them from immediately going on the defensive.

9. Make Time for Feedback.

Obtaining responses from direct reports are simple to delay, yet business culture can atrophy rapidly unless you preserve regular possibilities for feedback and training course correction. Be mindful not to allow these phone calls to slip into tactical work. The result is discovering directly regarding problems or concerns that might or else fly under supervisor radar, especially for staff members that tend to be more shy or introverted.

10. Get To The Source

If something goes askew, do not simply think somebody dropped the ball and start directing fingers. We start with the 5 Whys, a 10-min workout that can be done separately or as a group. You could discover that a functional issue requires to be resolved or that a staff member has an area for individual growth. Instead of just discovering a fall-guy when points fail, addressing the 5 Whys assists the team to recognize that you respect both business objectives and their personal development.

11. Help Them Unplug Entirely on Vacation

In our business, we make it possible for employees to get ready for their time off ahead of time and momentarily hand off all obligations so they can truly let go and unwind while vacationing. Each job is passed on to one more team member temporarily. As part of the hand-off, the visitor performs a quick phone call with everybody that will be covering for them. Authority, timelines, and various other products are that recorded in a shared log that any individual can access for advice on who to speak to. As a result, work continues to stream like a well-oiled device while the employee is away, and every person obtains the moment off they require with a peace of mind.

12. Remove the Remote So Often

Although the business globe has expanded rather comfy with the concept of remote work, you can not underestimate the power of hanging out together, face-to-face. We hold "team on sites" rather than offsite, and we treat it like a journey to the 1980s: the entire team gets off innovation and enjoy some human-to-human interaction. There are many positive results from the event in a common physical space. It assists in preparing long-term methods, boosting morale, building connections, and bringing brand-new hires into the layer. We have actually discovered people that do not adapt well to participating in a group on sites are hardly ever a great suitable for our company in the future.

LEAN START-UP IN THE HARD SCIENCES

Bringing the Little Start-up Way of Thinking to Huge Firms

Chris Thoen spent almost the whole of his 32-year occupation operating in scientific research and technology, and he's done so while deftly stabilizing in between benefiting large companies and little start-ups-- often finding methods to deal with both sorts of business at the same time. When he was fresh out of university, Chris's initial task went to a tiny biotech start-up in Belgium. It was not just an excellent shift from university life to professional life, yet it was a terrific intro to just how young business can really work.

After a few years, he desired more of a difficulty and the capability to constantly innovate on originalities, which led him to his next task at Procter & Gamble.

"Basically, every six months you [were] on a new project," Chris remembers, "You're doing something different and they're extending you as a scientist, or possibly as a supervisor."

The busy nature of the business matched Chris, and he invested the following number of decades of his career working with projects-- large and little-- for the firm. One of the highlights of his career was dealing with what he describes as basically a "start-up within the company" called Clay Street. For 12 weeks, he and 11 various other co- workers from various functions of the company, functioned solely on a solitary task. It's something that Chris still considers lovingly. "It was so equipping, so aspirational," he says. Most recently, he was the leader of science and innovation at Givaudan, the world's leading taste and sent home. While he was there, he came to be a founding partner of Mass Challenge Switzerland, an accelerator that takes no equity and assists start-ups to sharpen their organization and prepare their pitches for financiers. According to Chris, it is essential for big firms to locate means to ensure they continue to re-innovate and renew themselves with originalities.

"We intended to relate to start-up areas to obtain that stimulation ... that boost of energy for our very own monitoring team to truly see ... exactly how other individuals establish originalities and novel recommendations and exactly how you could collaborate to bring those concepts to the marketplace."

The Capability to Do 2 Things at Once

One of the principles Chris speaks in detail around is the concept of "ambidextrous leaders." For Chris, that implies leaders who are exceptionally good at handling their core organization while additionally being able to continue to think about fresh concepts and introduce wherefore customers need in the future.

"One point is without a doubt," Chris claims, "modification is upon us." And with that said, modification is the risk of falling behind by not locating ways to continue to discover, alter, grow, and introduce with the market. This is why Chris emphasizes, and it is necessary for the business to likewise have a level of ambidexterity to them. From his point of view, the best way for companies to do that is to have two different focuses on their business: the core side and the technology side. They stay within borders and concentrate on the daily success of the company. The development side, nevertheless, must be run entirely individually. The development site needs to be able to think openly in an exploratory and experimental method and, significantly, have the flexibility to stop working.

"For me, Failure is not an option," Chris states, "fall short is a phrase which stands for First Attempt in Knowing. Who doesn't wish to have an initial effort in discovering? If with those understandings, you can do your work much better afterward, so much the far better." According to Chris, it is necessary to keep both separate since it's difficult for people to efficiently do both jobs. There will frequently be open tasks for the core organization to consider, so introducing will be put to the back burner.

It's the ability to see the importance of both sides of the firm and to aid place systems in a position to bridge the interaction of the teams to maintain everyone aligned and favourably to work together. Likewise, discussing success and failings honestly. "Do not attempt to press the failings under the rug," he says, "however, actually use it as a knowing experience for the wider organization." When reviewing successes, it should not be self-congratulatory, yet rather, have to do with how it's aiding the company to grow.

The Value of Being Open to Ideas from Anywhere

Despite the appropriate leadership, Chris assumes that today's hectic market requires companies to remain to look beyond their own interior resources to innovate.

"In the past, it was the large companies consuming the little," Chris says, "nowadays, it's the fast consuming the slow-moving."

It does not make sense for firms to do whatever inside, anymore. It merely takes too much time, cash and resources. Companies should be looking beyond their very own walls-- and also their own market-- to continue to find new methods to help them become successful in the locations where they're attempting to prosper. That's not to state that it's easy. It does need the ideal state of mind, the capacity to see the favourable potential of an idea and then having the ability to see means to make it effective. It also needs the capability to focus on exactly how the suggestion can help the company, both for what it means currently and for what the firm might stand for in the future.

Chris suggests that large firms make certain they have their own house in order prior to decreasing the open technology course. It's critical to ensure that your company is internally prepared to get these brand-new possibilities and to understand exactly how to take care of them. For the smaller sized companies looking to introduce with larger firms, Chris suggests that you approach areas that are known to be sustained from the top monitoring. Likewise, to find out why individuals are encouraged to work with you-- figure out exactly how both sides profit, so you recognize what to anticipate with your partnership.

Make Development Part of Your Company Conversation

It's basically when individuals from within a company really feel threatened when ideas come from an outside source. In order to combat this, Chris recommends leaders reframe the attitude and make concepts not feel like a threat, however an opportunity. Employees should seem like they have the capacity to place their fingerprints on a project to assist the task come to be a success, even if the suggestion came from elsewhere. Still, not every employee is going to be fit for operating in innovation. There are particular people that aren't wired to believe by doing this, which's okay. "There's enough job to be done inside within a firm that you can put them in your own labs," Chris states.

On the other hand, there are individuals that are really sustained by the start-up mind-set and collaborating with individuals who come up with the new, insane suggestions.

"You have to assume [regarding] that you position in which type of setting," Chris claims, and afterward, you can develop from there. In order for any of that to be successful, empowerment and motivation need to start from the top. Leadership requires to set the instance and have expectations of advancement become part of the routine dialogue of the company. It makes it typical and non-threatening. It likewise permits individuals from all levels to really feel as though they have the possibility ahead up with the ideas. Since you never understand where the following big idea is most likely to originate from.

Believing Beyond
Conventional Wisdom

It can take a lot of money and time for a focused scientific research company to develop financial return for capitalists. For Jeff Uhlrig, the challenge of converting an innovative modern technology right into a satisfying opportunity for capitalists was an interesting obstacle and has actually been his focus since signing up with Sirrus in 2013.

In those five years, Jeff successfully commercialized and offered the firm. No tiny feat, according to Jason. "The conventional wisdom is that in this difficult science modern technology ... it's going to take ten, fifteen years and $200 million to show this product out, and get it out right into the marketplace.

Jeff had the ability to take a different approach to develop the company, and make it function, and produce excellent end results for the capitalists, and obtain an innovation that has a favourable effect on the globe out into the marketplace," Jason says. Most importantly, he did it in such a way that's repeatable by using concepts and techniques that are very sensible in high science markets and markets that surpass software program and consumer products.

The Importance of Being Unrelenting

For Jeff and Sirrus, locating success implied getting back to the basics of what they really felt customers and companions would certainly care about a lot of while functioning within their restricted spending plan. They quickly wrapped up that implied being clever in regard to how they invested their money. In their case, using it to develop a minimal feasible example-- not a full product. They delivered their item to prospective partners with a "highly technological plan" that notified them about the item and all of the things it can doing and then requested comments. This helped improve any guesswork at the same time and enabled them to focus their next enter creating the following iteration of a sensible example.

"We had the ability to create passion by ... only having one example. Then we just utilized that to notify future choices." The technique functioned, and they were able to generate solid and effective collaborations, yet it took a lot of jobs.

"You have to be ruthless," Jeff says," [My spreadsheet has] possibly over 1,000 names on it of people we've spoken with over the last five years." He estimates that they have about a 10% conversion rate from turning the samples they sent right into joint development partnerships.

Work with Individuals, Not Companies

That's not to say they weren't choosy. Sirrus was mindfully discerning concerning that they sent materials to and, much more importantly, how they cultivated their partnerships with partners. One of their initial requirements was locating individuals who were "intimately concentrated on intellectual property advancement," Jeff states, because it meant they were normally thinkers who such as resolving issues and assisting in establishing the innovation better. Finding those collaborations was crucial to Sirius' organization design. It not only aided Sirius to create their item additionally. However, it permitted those companies to file copyright and be first to the marketplace, making use of Sirius' unique item.

Their crucial standards in looking for partners are finding fantastic people to deal with. "Our experience is that people and companies are not associated whatsoever," Jeff says. Due to the fact that companies are large entities, and even if one person isn't curious about your innovation doesn't mean someone else in the business will not. That's why Jeff succeeds in pursuing a highly communicative, "multi-pronged technique" within a company. Sirrus works carefully with individuals on every degree of a firm's organizational graph, from the most degrees to the CTO.

Dimensions of Success

A firm's success can't be gauged on relationships alone. According to Jeff, it is very important to maintain a concentrate on your goals and what you want your utmost result to be. For Sirrus, they wanted two things: to produce a purposeful departure for their financiers and to ensure their innovation obtained commercialized and given the market. The very first was the "ruthless focus on intellectual property development." Jeff believes that "in order to have an effective exit," they required patents that were worldwide released, not simply pending. It's something that they track each and every single month. The second statistic, the one they were most carefully concentrated on, was their consumer fostering cycle.

"What it actually [comes] down to is somebody devoted on paper ... that they're going to appoint sources," Jeff says, "in a lot of cases, they assign considerable dollars to the collaboration." Lastly, their 3rd statistics-- unquestionably something that's not as quantifiable-- was the metric of a team. "A large part of the process ... is that [your team is]," Jeff says. They were diligent concerning locating the right people to hire for each setting. Since, when purchasers can be found in, they'll talk with every team member. Jeff thinks it is essential for [the buyers] to really feel that no actual changes to the group dynamic are required. "We utilized [just how the team is assembled and working] as a huge part of our evaluation.

UTILIZING LEAN START-UP TO LAUNCH AND SCALE POLITICAL CAMPAIGNS

Producing a Better Means to Project

When it concerns political campaigns, Dante Vitagliano wants to develop a great company. When he and his companions started Pinnacle Campaign Techniques, they laid out to fix some of the problems they constantly saw occurring in political campaigns.

Improving the 3 Political Phases

Dante has recognized three major phases in the political procedure where he believes the Lean Start-up technique can help campaigners do a better job In the pre-launch phase, candidates talk with people around them to get support. Typically, prospects think everything is working out since they're basing it on feelings and hearing what they wish to hear. Dante believes that candidates need to be much more organized in their technique. They should have more concrete solutions and measurable metrics at this stage, like recognizing the number of individuals is most likely to contribute money to their project.

"This is something that [programs] you can be a practical prospect, and there's some proof to back it up,"

The second stage-- the launch stage-- is where prospects ought to be identifying their minimal sensible product. Dante explains that it does not take much to obtain your name on the ballot-- anybody can file paperwork to do this. What prospects truly need to be a reputable competitor is a message, an area where people can see that message, and a method to gather donations. If you have those points, you can get to the 3rd phase: scaling.

Knowing and Measuring in Modern Campaigns

Trial and error, learning, and rotating are Lean Start-up hallmarks that can also be implemented in political campaigns. If no one respects the prospect's major issues, preferably, you should take the lesson from your target market and pivot onto something else. This means Dante sees it, and there is a great deal of means prospects can gain from their audiences.

In the past, intelligence would certainly be gathered from a large-scale study. However, there are intrinsic biases in that process. These studies can additionally be quite pricey. Another way political campaigns are able to accumulate data is through social listening. The social network provides candidates the devices to obtain continual responses loophole. If they structure their content well, they can obtain real insights right into what's resonating-- or otherwise reverberating-- with their target markets. Through this procedure, they can experiment to see what messages are reverberating and working.

Dante explains that today, there are plenty of tools that help measure every little thing from messaging to create components to even the layout of an email. You have to be conscientious concerning the method of testing these experiments. Otherwise you encounter what Dante calls "pasta chucking, when you're simply tossing spaghetti against the wall and waiting to see what sticks," which isn't a mindful or reliable strategy.

The Course to Making Purposeful Change

Inevitably, Dante thinks that the Lean Start-up method can be advantageous not simply to services, yet to any individual aiming to make a distinction and has the potential to be really helpful for candidates.

"I like to assume that if we're much more disciplined in the means, we construct our projects, then we'll be doing ourselves an excellent solution." Political professionals and even the campaigns themselves are really comparable to the start-up globe. It is very important that they recognize that anticipating analytics and forecasting can just obtain them up until now and that they can make better gains by examining their strategies and rotating and adapting where needed.

"We're here to win elections," Dante states, "and we do that because we really hope that individuals that we elect can create purposeful adjustment somehow. Similar to a start-up with a vision to transform the means people do any kind of company, I think that Lean Start-up provides us a chance to transform the manner in which people recognize and approach politics."

A Unique Option to a Productivity Problem

Pushkar Kale began needing to be far from work for hours each time during moms and dad meetings for his child's institution admission. He was reviewing this obstacle with his (currently) service companion, that has his very own production business, and agreed the process was particularly hard. In the production world, it's tough-- if not difficult-- for supervisors to be away from the factory and keep points running efficiently, so he would certainly need to frequently be on his phone.

Going Slow to Prevent Going As Well Fast

Even though his companion had a production company and enjoyed the suggestion, they decided to "take conscious actions." Pushkar had been complying with Lean Start-up for a long time.

"The major takeaway for me," he claims, "is that we often tend to fall in love with our own ideas." But liking your concept excessive can cause moving on as well rapidly, inevitably causing "failing or calamity." They progressed by talking with their prospective clients:

manufacturing managers. They consulted with more than twenty different firms under a range of domain names. Their discussions not only validated their initial suggestion, however likewise helped they determine methods to improve upon it before they even created a single line of code.

Many of the business they talked to like the concept of having the information offered; however, required a budget-friendly way to capture the information behind what's happening on their shop floor. With their client research study in hand, they prepared their first minimum feasible product: Excel-based documents with a data entrance screen and dashboard. They handed the easy file to their possible customers and accumulated their comments. With the details they got, Pushkar and his companion were able to identify which of their assumptions were right and where they required to pivot their reasoning. One crucial pivot came right as they will start product development. They thought that their software application would be utilized on smartphones. Nonetheless, numerous companies don't permit cell phones on the production line for safety purposes. They took this note in stride and created a system where information could be gotten in by utilizing centrally located tablets instead. It's a model that is being used today and, according to Pushkar, is "working smoothly."

Your Individuals Are Your Foundation.

Today, as Trixware Technologies begins to scale, Pushkar is striving to ensure they're establishing themselves up for success. For him, that suggests placing a heavy concentrate on his group-- his people-- rather than procedures and tools.

"If your group is in place, you can scale to any kind of wonderful level," he describes, noting that the capability to share their understanding with a brand-new staff member is vital to their success. That does not suggest they're not considering their product or service. As they scale up, they're working with growing their "technological intricacy," too, by offering numerous variations of their product: standard, sophisticated, and enterprise degrees. This will enable them to attract various segments of the sector to reach a broader consumer base.

A Great Partnership Results In Wonderful Success.

Pushkar happily connects the success they have actually had thus far to their use of Lean Start-up tools and strategies. He believes that if they would certainly approach the issue in otherwise, they would have wound up with a product that would just serve to a handful of individuals, and they would not have actually seen the development and growth they have today. He additionally offers credit history to the joint means he and his partner approached this task and their partnership. They entered into the business with clearly defined boundaries.

Given that his partner worked in production, he took the lead on finding out what would certainly be required to enhance the day-to-day operations in a manufacturing centre. With his history in software application and IT, Pushkar would figure out how these things would be carried out. Reflecting on their last couple of years, Pushkar reviews things that he's discovered along the way. His suggestions to budding business owners are "rather than focusing on what "wows," concentrate on what truly works and what is really required." He assumes that it's easy to try to find the "wow" consider a suggestion early on, however before you do that, you must have a solid understanding of what the end-users need. From there, you can construct and fine-tune your idea right into a product that you can offer.

LEAN ITEM ADVANCEMENT AND HOW TO SELECT THE RIGHT VALUE RECOMMENDATION

Polish Your MVP

Lars swiftly realized that while an MVP is a fundamental part of the customer screening and recognition procedure, particularly for established firms, "it requires to be polished. You cannot really de-scope the final product whatsoever so as to get it out much faster." Lars stated this means you need to generate "creative means to get client feedback throughout your item cycle also prior to you go out with the full launch."

Positioning is Key

While the MVP is necessary, Lars stated they invest the vast majority of their recognition on their product cycle, especially on what he calls "placing." In short, this boils down to: "Just how are we offering?

Don't Depend On Your Instinct; Speak To the Customer

Lars, after that, supplied an unusual admission when he said that he has discovered not to trust his instinct in this procedure. Actually, relying on instinct has actually led him astray.

"Every single time I attempt to shortcut the process, I constantly get burned." Relying on one's instinct commonly implies not listening to the consumer, he clarified. "Until I've obtained hands on. I try not to make a lot of assumptions concerning what would work [have] no assumptions and identify who I'm speaking with." From there, he begins with a common survey and common client evaluations, "The kind of things that you actually do if you were trying to develop a company or you're running a start-up for the first time."

Usage Abdominal Muscle Screening and Ranking Studies

Lars has found out to place a lot of faith in the client's capacity to establish what products or features are excellent. He makes use of AB screening, placing a number of different options before consumers, and inquiring which ones they're most delighted concerning and willing to spend for.

"Individuals are a pretty good judge of whether ... it suffices," Lars stated. Moreover, what they like is commonly counterintuitive. "I am continually surprised concerning what success." Lars has actually had a lot of success supplying what he calls "ranking studies," which he called a "really simple way to get genuine data behind these value proposals." In them, they supply 5-7 alternatives of valuable suggestions for brand-new functions they're thinking about. There's no magic response to obtaining that value recommendation right, other than to keep doing customer interviews, which Lars stated is less complicated than it might seem. "My group has done hundreds literally. Otherwise, thousands of these points ... and I have never ever had trouble obtaining individuals to agree to a telephone call."

Soft Launch an MVP

Once they have a strong idea, from customer meetings, what the product requires to be, they produce a limited MVP that he contrasted to "a very early accessibility program or a soft launch that a technology company may do." As an example, instead of the complete eight-week course, they'll use a two-hour, paid webinar on the same standard curriculum, dramatically de-scoped to a limited audience of around 20 people.

"The main thing we're always trying to find ... is exactly how quickly does it sell out?" When the value recommendation is right, the places "simply go out the door and quickly sell out." If not, they reassess.

Falls at the End of the Process

When products are close to launching, Lars claimed there is still a usage for the waterfall strategy. "We start writing all the scripts for the last variation of the product. We start putting together all the PDFs." Also there they confirm by inviting a pick group of customers to be on an advising council to provide comments on the items.

"We make sure there are no kinks, anything vital that individuals are stumbling over that's going to get in the means of the final launch."

Keys to Building Better Products

Vasily Starostenko enjoys troubles. Today he leads the customer purchase group at Tesla, and before that, he was an item manager on the driver team at Uber. At both firms, he's learned that effective items start with an unrelenting concentrate on fixing client problems.

1. Understand: Stay Clear of Attribute Proclivity by Starting with an Issue Statement.

Vasily knows that it is very easy for firms to succumb to feature fetish: "When we just release a function, and we celebrate the feature launch, it typically happens that we do not even ever clearly talk about what problem was it released to resolve? What problems has it really resolved?" If you can't answer these concerns, then you're most likely not building lasting items.

An easy means to guarantee you're focused on consumers, not features, is to start the item cycle with an "explicit trouble declaration," and it should be "from the customer's viewpoint," not the company's, "since your firm exists and your item exists to satisfy the consumer requirement," shares Vasily. As an example, the dilemma needs to not be exactly how the business can expand new individuals by 20 percent due to the fact that "clients perhaps want your business to stay alive and use good items, but they do not really desire the company to expand." Development is not a consumer need. Yet, what do consumers need? Identifying the right (and actual) customer problem is difficult. "It's important to determine the issue. "How exactly you do it? There is no clear victor," Vasily admits. He does, nevertheless, have a couple of tips.

First, he recommends checking out at the very least 50 troubles before deciding to fix one. He also believes that the Double Ruby design version works for helping groups to decide where to concentrate.

2. Experiment: "Always Have a Hypothesis," But do not be blinded by Science.

You may assume you've recognized clear trouble, but as Vasily has actually found out, "often you're reviewing trouble that doesn't also exist." To avoid addressing phantom problems, Vasily emphasizes that you should "constantly have a theory." A hypothesis pressures you to focus on what you anticipate results to be if you have actually properly identified the trouble, and those outcomes ought to be quantifiable. To measure, you have to identify metrics that you will certainly use to figure out if the item test was successful.

Vasily states that you need to identify every experiment a success or failure, or as he says, every experiment has to be "called." Even though "calling" an experiment depends heavily on quantitative proof, Vasily worries that you can't be as well focused on numbers. "Information shows you the past. To comprehend the future you need to be always thinking about qualitative procedures. Talk with your consumers.

Figure [out] what happens in customer support." To verify his point, he recounts his experience attempting to urge Uber drivers to drive more hrs.

His team created a function that asked, "Are you certain you intend to go offline?" and motivated chauffeurs with messages such as "You're 15 mins short of 5 hrs" or "If you end up now, you will certainly complete at trip number 9. How around you drive one more journey?" Vasily keeps in mind that "individuals consequently drove method more," yet ultimately, the attribute was discontinued since, despite the fact that some motorists were driving more, several were annoyed by the attribute.

"The variety of hours you drive is really not the right success statistics due to the fact that it's just revealing you currently what's occurring. It's not showing you what's going to occur tomorrow. Suppose all these upset people, tomorrow, simply don't come?" Vasily describes that a basic means to make certain that you speak with customers that might be frustrated by a function is to consist of a way for consumers to allow you to know, "I despise this function."

An internet marketer metric is one method to measure clients' love (and hate) for a brand-new product, but ultimately, Vasily says, "As high as you want to construct science, the human judgment cannot be replaced by just a set of procedures." You wish to make sure you have an item team with "good judgment," which you "talk to your customers constantly."

3. Align: Put Your Money Where Your Mouth Is

Placement is making your company around having the effect you have actually confirmed with experiments, or as Vasily describes, placing your cash where your mouth is. He supplies the instance of Uber: "Uber has a driver team and a cyclist group. It makes good sense because there are vehicle drivers, and there are cyclists. And when I was there, the development team quit existing." Chauffeurs and motorcyclists were focused on.

Focusing on and intending help construct a company lined up for impact. Vasily is quick to estimate Mike Tyson, "Every person has a strategy till they get typed the face," but, he states, "Still have a plan." Vasily believes that the planning process assists organizations in prioritizing and prevent inner miscommunication.

"When there are numerous teams, those teams often clash about, should I be solving this problem, or should you be resolving this trouble?" The plan will certainly assist you "determine which team is addressing which part of the consumer requirement." Once plans and top priorities are developed, the punches will certainly come, and things will certainly alter, but staying concentrated on the client problem need to help maintain your teams aligned.

Vasily is "constantly clearly discuss what troubles we are addressing" also "with each and every single non-product and a non-tech team that I engage." He believes that "when it's apparent [that] I'm trying to make my customers happier by doing this, it's more likely to obtain the same to the ultimate group which will be applying it." Vasily states, "Communication straightens out in your organization when you discuss problems."

WHAT'S CURRENTLY ON THE MINDS OF ENTREPRENEURS?

Helping the Present and Seeking To the Future of Start-ups

In 2004, Theron McCollough signed up with a start-up and never ever recalled. He has actually remained in the start-up space ever since. As the Managing Director of the Beginning Technique at Silicon Valley Bank (SVB), his primary task is "simply aiding start-ups." He gets to link business and individuals with each other and help make the intros that particularly match with what start-up creators are constructing. "It's what makes me get up on a daily basis," Theron says, "and I'm delighted to find to use." In his duty at Silicon Valley Bank, among the things Theron gets to deal with is the Start-up Expectation Record they launch every year.

Good Aid can be Difficult to Locate

Every firm, large or little, has to take care of working with on some degree, so it's not shocking that 82% of the start-ups that SVB talked with the wish to enhance their labour force (see web page 10 of the record). However, the report reveals intriguing insight on just how challenging these start-ups believed it was to locate employees with the abilities to grow their service: 29% found it extremely tough, 62% located it rather difficult, and 9% believed it had not been very difficult. Theron chalks these percentages approximately trends in the marketplace, and the kinds of company's people want to benefit. The firms in the 9% brace are more than likely in areas like AI or block chain that are most likely to be extra interesting or might be elevating more resources. Even if the business isn't the very best executing on the market, individuals they work with still obtain the benefit of getting experience and finding out so much in these new and interesting spaces. While the other industries "are very intriguing [and interesting]," Theron says, from an employing viewpoint, "There's less quantity to pick from."

Women are recovering their lost achievement in Leadership Duties
Several of the most encouraging data on the report worried ladies in management positions. The percent of people start-ups with at least one lady on the board of supervisors raised to 37 percent (from 29 percent in 2018), and at least one woman in an executive setting boosted by ten portions indicate 53%. If the percent continues to continuously boost over the next 3 to five years, could that create more balance for these businesses? He keeps in mind that, in the past, having individuals in the office who originate from different histories and various viewpoints have helped companies flourish.

Raising Funds May be Less difficult

Among the info that Theron discovered intriguing was just how start-ups watched raising funds. Much more interesting is that one-quarter of those start-ups state the fundraising environment is not tough. Theron liquid chalks a great deal of this as much as the enhanced existence of information. "There's more data for both the investment neighbourhood along with the start-up neighbourhood," he states. Those companies who can gather data that confirm the accuracy of their product or service will certainly find it less challenging to increase funds. There may be even more money going around, but that it's most likely to companies that have actually shown product-market fit and have actually proven some type of profits. Business that are pre-seed or are seed firms without any proven market fit or lower incomes normally has a harder time increasing funds because the money is most likely to more well-known business.

A Makeover at Long Term Goals

A majority of start-ups say that their long-term goal is to be acquired. Yet it's a smaller percentage that is perhaps extra fascinating. Theron explains that this may be because there are a lot more choices for business currently. The various other points he's observing is business who wish to keep or have control of their company. "Once you elevate the rate round on an institutional round, you can shed that degree of control," he states. Creators are thinking about all choices before dropping any particular route.

The Most Promising New Sectors

This is something that Theron mirrors. "We're really doing some deep technology that's making a purposeful distinction," he claims, "I believe there's going to be a whole lot a lot more investments by doing this."

Looking at the longer-term-- a decade from now-- entrepreneurs believe that self-governing transportation has the opportunity to make the greatest jump in perspective, whereas that sector does not also make the leading five listings for today. This isn't as well unexpected, with personal, commercial, and freight markets all standing to take advantage of breakthroughs in technology and technology. Probably throughout the next ten years, laws will certainly loosen up, and people will certainly be extra open up to autonomous transportation as an industry. Theron additionally keeps in mind Life Sciences, which was available in 3rd on the listing of developments with one of the most guarantee for the future, is a fascinating topic.

5 CRITIQUES OF LEAN START-UP AND WHY THEY DON'T STAND UP

Do not get me wrong. I believe that providing useful objection on any type of subject is excellent. Absolutely nothing needs to be considered approved. Only with examining, discussing and constructive review that brings about brand-new understandings can we boost. I really hope that this blog post, and any remarks that might come as a result, offers one small step in that direction.

1. "Having a solid technique is more vital than carrying out lots of market tests."

This normally begs the question, what is meant by a "solid approach." Without specifying generic statements, we have no clear foundation of where to even start to take on an issue. What is suggested by "strong," and how can we know when it's "strong"? Vision or objective ought to direct direction, while the method needs to adjust to understandings and adjustments in the setting. This implies that we must agree to question our method, which is in-line with a data- driven lean start-up mind-set. Our function, which ought to resonate with our individual beliefs and values is the last point that must transform. Although lean start-up goes much deeper than running experiments to in/validate assumptions, the lean start-up has the ability to educate not only methods but approach too. It's not that "technique" is more crucial than "lean start-up," they ought to go together.

2. "We don't believe more recognition is better. We evaluated it, and it doesn't work for us."

This, and variations of the very same, are timeless instances of knocking a method since it does not deliver the anticipated results, as opposed to questioning if you're doing a bad job of using the approach. In a lean start-up, there are pitfalls to keep an eye out for, e.g., "vanity metrics" and "incorrect validation." Allowing on your own get off course by complying with non-actionable metrics, or assuming that you obtained recognition when you didn't, are examples of inadequate application of the technique. A lot more specifically, asking closed-ended questions such as "Do you like our item" with the customer reacting "yes," does not equivalent recognition. The customer might just wish to obtain you out of his workplace and will certainly say anything that accomplishes this objective.

The entrepreneur takes the "yes" as fantastic news and extrapolates this even better when debriefing the team. Obtaining recognition for things that the client does not care about or confusing what someone claims with what they will really do, is not the correct application of lean start-up. In lean start-up, we do not just take on the task of screening everything that moves. We prioritize what we test for, watch out for untold prejudice, discover wise ways to develop our experiments to elicit one of the most beneficial understandings with the least amount of resources-- and we require to determine what gets determined. It's a tall order; however, dismissing an approach out of control that generates concrete results for plenty of others might not be the best method.

3. "Doing client interviews or consumer growth does not benefit us."

You probably haven't dug deep enough to understand the issues your clients are dealing with and the contextualized outcomes or end results that they are attempting to achieve. You also may not have not rated the results according to relevance. If you have been through a couple of interviews and then go straight to developing your MVP and running quantitative examinations, I would certainly not be shocked if consumer development doesn't deliver the results that you had expected. A common mistake is to bundle issue and service discovery interviews into the identical interview, giving rise to a variety of other troubles.

4. "Too much feedback from consumers might trigger the business

owners to alter the concept so regularly that they come to be disheartened."

That's why the group has to prioritize what to take in and what to dispose of. Groups that jump about excessive based on consumer responses need aid from skilled advisors to specify their function and vision. They need to discover what metrics to focus on, which in turn is dependent on the business model, and each level of the start-up remains in.

Lean start-up is not regarding "rotating" all the time—Vice versa. If you're constantly rotating, you're refraining lean start-up, you're doing the chicken dance. The lean start-up has to do with being data-driven, or data-informed, rather than letting viewpoints determine your following step. It's about evaluating your most risky assumptions beforehand, and in essence, concentrating on finding something worth structure, before spending resources right into actually building and scaling.

5. "The lean start-up method may be producing "false negatives,"

suggesting good ideas are incorrectly turned down since the technique does not have a clear regulation for when entrepreneurs and entrepreneurs ought to state success, stop screening, and begin scaling production."

There are no "off-the-shelf" clear policies to adhere to. These are created and chosen by the group. However, there are lots of standards, devices, and inspiration that other lean start-up professionals share. Exactly how do you recognize if it's a "good concept" unless you test it? Moreover, business owners must never ever stop testing, also when scaling. If you're rotating at all times, you're simply not dealing with lean start-up the right way. In today's fast relocating globe, the timeless 5-year strategy is dead! The significance of the approach is choosing what not to do. The wonderful aspect of a lean start-up is that if you start to use it in a self-disciplined style, and according to ideal methods, it will assist you in determining what your approach needs to be.

What's wrong with the lean start-up technique?

For the inexperienced, the Lean Start-up method is a method for developing products and organizations based upon 'confirmed discovering,' getting client feedback promptly and frequently. This method has changed the means companies are established. Rather than building alone from users, start-ups on a regular basis reveal the product to customers throughout the advancement cycle. In doing so, groups are able to make even smarter decisions concerning what to build, from core item works to what colour a button should be. This appears reasonable, typical sensual, and is really practical planned of digital organisations.

When the method is repackaged, it is oversimplified

As more people begin to think that entrepreneurship is the option to their corporate troubles, more items emerge to educate people in exactly how to end up being entrepreneurs. It is not unexpected then that the approach has actually been repackaged, repurposed and resold in 'entrepreneurship courses' that guarantee to aid you to make '$ 1000 a month. Much of these are by effective, legitimate business owners and a great deal of them meet their guarantees. In efforts to transform the lean way of thinking into workable actions, they frequently generate advice that is restrictive. For instance, the preferred strategy of developing a touchdown web page interacting the trouble and proposed solution, consisting of a sign-up sheet or approach to pay, then running a Google AdWords project may be sufficient for a confirming whether or not to proceed with a taxi application or an e-book on fish maintaining. It could show enormously not enough for a team wanting to begin a luxury resort to acquire any significant info about exactly how to wage their organization. The drive to be marginal can cause entrepreneurs to think about giving up on high quality when they shouldn't.

Businesses like Ikawa, manufacturers of the electronic mini coffee roaster needed to help years up until they had a shippable model. In talks with their owner, Andrew Stordy, he pointed out that "the extra physical a product obtains, the less lean item advancement can be." For a marketplace selling sports apparel, a page with phony images and a way for consumers to pay might be sufficient. Occasionally we intend to make things not because they can be 'confirmed' promptly, yet merely since we intend to transform our mind's vision into a fact. In some cases, regularly asking for a point of views can be preventative. Sometimes we may be required to work the various other methods around-- beginning with what we want to make and locating individuals who love it rather than figuring out precisely what people desire us to make and after that making it.

The lean start-up technique is something that educates what I make as an individual and exactly how we develop as a group. It informs the decision-making procedure, aiding us to come to be cleverer, focussing time and resources in the ideal location. Every market and every product growth process, digital or not, has something to extract from the lean start-up approach. In a lifetime Where we see creativity flourish, even beyond innovation, it is unsurprising that this methodology-- which was created with digital item advancement in mind-- is being layered onto the production procedures of non-digital items. Regardless of what you are building, whether it be an app or a plane, I advise you to accept not just the subtleties of product production but likewise the nuances of your inspirations to develop.

HOW LEAN START-UP APPROACHES RELATE TO NON-TECH SMALL COMPANY

The typical trajectory of concept, put together a group, construct an item, market the item and offer it as hard as you can have confirmed to be a dish for failing in today's hectic affordable service setting. Large and costly blunders are made when this type of hit-or-miss new product introduction procedure. The big idea isn't confirmed in the industry, Market behaviours, demands and desires are usually misjudged and what might have come to be an engaging business.

In 2008 US-based technology start-ups have made use of the lean start-up processes described by Eric Reis, Steve Blank and Alexander Osterwalder. It is a system that values trial and error over preparation, market feedback over instinct and a repetitive method to product advancement rather than a belief that if completely constructed, the consumers will come. The ever before evolving lean canvas has changed the established company plan. Instead of assuming that the thought of the company version will certainly work, the lean system looks for a business version that functions based on real evidence. It is said that service strategies hardly ever endure the first contact with clients. They frequently don't act in the method you think they will.

Boxer Mike Tyson expressed this truth most colourfully when he claimed, "Everyone has a strategy until they obtain punched in the mouth." The exact same holds true for small company proprietors and the consumers they desire to offer. Small company proprietors can take advantage of the lean start-up principles and procedures utilized by tech business owners to build and deliver wonderful items to thousands, otherwise millions, of clients rapidly and economically.

Below are three methods you can take advantage of tech lean start-up concepts to improve your local business today:

1. Verify Presumptions to Minimize Threat

The primary distinction between the old well-known routes to organization success is that the lean start-up entrepreneur first asks, "Should this suggestion be brought to market?" as opposed to "Just how do I develop my product?" List all of the presumptions you have regarding yourself. Include what you believe it will set you back to develop your item, who it will certainly benefit most, exactly how you will certainly drive recognition to your big idea and how you will offer it. Then develop little experiments to evaluate your concept.

For instance, if you're thinking of beginning a food truck company selling meat pies, you could easily and affordably launch a basic landing web page introducing that your "Meat Pie Food Vehicle" is coming quickly and a spot for people to enter in their email address if they want to be informed when it shows up in their location. You could then run a collection of Facebook ads to drive targeted traffic to your landing web page and assess the number of individuals who enrol in the announcement. The project could run for ten days at $5 each day. If no person registers, you may intend to rethink your idea or test with a better worth proposal or ad "hook" to inspire interest and the click via to the landing page. Beginning checking the assumptions that are the riskiest to your service practicality.

2. Talk to Your Market

Among the largest factors company, owner struggle is that they consider their organization and their item from their very own point of view. The trouble with that method is that the marketplace does not consider your organization and product the means you do. They each have their very own viewpoints. In order to figure out, especially exactly how your market thinks about your firm and what you have to offer, you need to speak with them. Google does not have your answers. You need to escape your work desk and go to where lots of people in your market can be found. You may discover teams of them at assemble. They could be patronizing the shopping mall. Find out what they share in the sorts of areas and events they participate in and get your butt over there. Ask open-ended inquiries regarding the relevant troubles they have, what pisses them off, what creates the greatest discomfort in their life or work. Seek to find out. Dig deep to totally understand their perspective influence of the trouble (discomfort), what difference it would certainly make to have a service (benefit) and what's working and not working concerning the things they are currently making use of to attempt to address the trouble. Just find out as much as you can.

3. Begin with a Minimum Viable Item

Instead of wasting much time, energy, and money in completely creating your item, simply develop the simplest and tiniest version of it to examine to see if you're headed in the appropriate direction. Analyse the comments you enter your initial talks with individuals in your market. Recognize the most important point your product has to do to supply the benefit your market is actively looking for. As an example, if you're the meat pie food truck visionary, one of the essential points might be that your meat pie tastes really great. Make a couple of pies and discover ways to do some preference screening with individuals that do not know and like you. Simply put, loved ones don't count. Their responses will likely be prejudiced. Solicit straightforward viewpoints from lots and great deals of people. Gather and analyse what they needed to claim and repeat from there. You might find that your consumers prefer to have the ability to grab your meat pies at the regional supermarket as opposed to waiting on a food truck to get here in their area.

The ongoing repeating of continued product development based upon a continuous customer feedback loop is what will get you to the holy grail of what is referred to as product-market fit. What this suggests is that you have a product that you recognize, as opposed to hoping your customers will like and buy at a profitable cost. Using technology, lean start-up planning and advancement processes in non-tech local business development guarantees that threats are reduced, large and costly blunders are avoided and ensures that the business has the flexibility and agility it requires to grow in a busy, every transforming, affordable marketplace.

Device Reimbursement - Lean Start-up Application

A whole lot has been discussed just how Lean Start-up methodology may aid entrepreneurs in building successful clinical gadget companies. In this write-up, we give a real-life failing instance of among our clients and suggest a process to execute the Lean Start-up technique to reduce the probability of such failures.

1. The Issue

Over the last seven years, we went seeking advice from services to more than 150 various clinical gadget start-ups. The depressing fact is that the majority of them stopped working. They fell short since they did not take care to give the market a readily successful item before running out of cash. Note they were successful in offering market all types of really innovative items, yet such that nobody was willing to spend for.

2. A the Real World Example

One of our clients developed a cutting-edge product, which contained a selection of electronic stethoscopes that passively keep an eye on resonance power. The product allowed medical professionals to keep track of sites of airway obstruction without subjecting the person to radiation or invasive procedures. The firm carried out a scientific study that showed the accuracy of its system and obtained the FDA's clearance with the planned use "keeping an eye on lung sounds." Now they approached us and asked that we help them create their repayment approach and execute it in the United States.

After doing some research, we interviewed a number of US payer agents that instantly informed us that: "It is going to be a cool day in hell before we spend for this innovation!" Had the item assisted clinicians set apart in between Bronchial asthma and COPD, they would certainly consider it, yet because they don't see what different professional decisions could be made by "keeping an eye on lung noises," they won't pay for it. Apparently, a great deal of monitoring and engineering effort and time were spent on choosing, making, creating, and examining attributes that of their stakeholders (payers) were not going to pay for. In order to develop a brand-new variation, differentiating in between Bronchial asthma and COPD, a large piece of the job was gotten rid of, in addition to performing a new medical research study and obtaining a new FDA clearance.

3. Applying Lean Start-up Technique

Lean Start-up supplies a few standard tools, one of which recommends developing an item incrementally and iteratively. As necessary, instead of developing, testing, getting FDA clearance, and only after that getting payers' responses, our customer over needs to have looked for payers' responses a whole lot earlier. Just how could any person get a payer's responses prior to the product is total? This is where Lean Start-up presents the idea of a minimal sensible item (MVP).

An MVP is the version of a brand-new product that permits the collection of stakeholders' comments. We call the MVP that we establish for our customers a 'Pseudo File' This 'Pseudo File' includes a lot of the paperwork the firm anticipates to obtain in the future, once the item is fully developed and cleared/approved for advertising and marketing. It is based on the company's estimates, not the actual information.

The included pseudo data may indicate approximated clinical test results, product prices, etc. Adhering to the development of this 'Pseudo Dossier,' payers might become close to at onset and asked to discuss the 'Pseudo File' as if it was based upon real information (anticipated just within a year or more). Their comments might be made use of to 'Pivot,' i.e., make changes to the business's product, application, or professional strategy at the very beginning, reducing the creation of waste and increasing the opportunities of developing a readily effective product before running out of money.

4. Establishing a 'Pseudo Dossier.'

When we develop a 'Pseudo File,' we commonly take the adhering to steps:

- Draft a Value Story, which tells us how making use of the new device gives medical and financial benefits contrasted to the existing options.
- Create an Economic Design, quantifying the economic advantages, and enabling sensitivity evaluation.
- Validating that existing scientific data sustain the medical and economic claims in the Worth Story and Economic Version or adding repayment associated aspects to any type of scheduled scientific study

procedure, along with the business's estimated outcomes.

The above Worth Tale, Economic Design and existing/planned scientific information (consisting of the approximated outcomes) are presented to pertinent doctors and payers, seeking their feedback as if the product is full and the estimated scientific research results represent the actual outcomes that may be obtained within a year or two.

In case of negative feedback, the business must consider altering the Value Story, Economic Version, clinical information, or item and after that, seek payers' feedback again up until getting positive feedback. Just upon invoice of favourable comments, it would make sense to proceed with the advancement job and scientific research. Otherwise it is simply a pricey gamble which might result in the firm's failure.

HOW TO MAINTAIN CAPITAL POSITIVE AS A BUSINESS START-UP

One of the biggest difficulties for any organization start-up is the ability to have favourable capital at all times throughout the year. When times obtain lean, and revenues decrease, you can really feel a pinch in your working resources and need a method to construct these monetary gets back up to their top. The reverse applies when earnings are rising, and you are making bank - you really feel the valuable weight of some included funds sitting in your cash flow gets all set to be spent. However, you need to level this cyclical trend with a favourable capital all year-round. Right here are some methods you can keep your working resources positive throughout your sales cycle.

Stop Overspending

Among the easiest methods to obtain your cash flow in check is to quit spending too much when the need is truly not there. This can aid you to have the cash you need when a concern emerges without having to battle to find up with the financing.

Remain on Top of Invoicing

Making money for the job you have actually finished is an arduous task for any start-up. It is no fun chasing down late repayments, yet it is your duty as an organization start-up owner to see to it your invoicing goes out in a timely manner and makes money.

Track your day to day Expenses

You might require to reign in your expenses; however, without tracking them, you have no way of understanding where your cash flow is going every day.

Maintain a record of all the expenditures you make every single day and examine them to see where you can cut down. You might be making unnecessary purchases that are costing are building up and affecting your working capital.

Keep a Cushion

If you understand your business start-up has a hard time from time-to-time with its capital, you can prepare for these times by setting aside a cushion of funds that you can depend on when you require it. This can make your slower months less made complex to birth and also give you a strong publication that you can depend on when an emergency occurs. It can supply you some consisted of security that you have the funds when revenues dip.

Quote Future Earning Conservatively

When you look ahead, it can be really simple to overestimate what your earning will definitely be the list below year. You might anticipate sales that are not satisfactory, or unforeseen scenarios might hold. To maintain your good cash flow, be sensible in your future profits and prepare for the unexpected, so you don't end up in a situation where your working capital vanishes without cautioning.

Boost Sales

While it goes without saying that enhancing your sales can aid you in expanding your capital, yet this is one area that service start-ups can delay. Consider the manner in which you can include value to your offerings and lure customers to get more than ever before. Packages and add-ons are simple means to obtain a customer to invest more with you and aid boost your sales in any type of provided month.

Secure a Short-Term Capitalist

Short-term angel financiers are a fool proof way to start your business start-up and get the funding you require to aid with your capital troubles. They can offer financing when times are tough and allow you to breathe a little much easier with their financial backing. A short-term angel investor can offer you cash to grow your organization while still maintain the daily circulation. Paid back over a shorter quantity of time, these seed financiers aid to provide you a lot more adaptability and provide different methods of securing financing for your organization start-up.

Develop Loyal Consumers

Transforming your consumers into devoted followers that regularly your company regularly can help you expand sales and boost your earnings all throughout the year. These repeat consumers can provide you company start-up the boost it needs while likewise helping your capital to swell with each acquisition. When you can rely on a client to go back to your business, not just does it guarantee one more sale.

Keep Stock Lean

Making sure that you do not overflow your supply. That can stop a negative cash flow for your start-up service. Practice being lean and just have the stock you need at any kind of provided time. This can make a difference in your service' profits and boost your capital circumstance. Having items and products handy might be nice, yet you will certainly find that your procedures are just as effective, and you are not waiting months to offer your backlog, impacting your monthly working capital.

Workflow Administration and the Start-up Company

What's the product? Does it exist on the market? Where is the preliminary funding coming from? How seasoned is the administration team? These are a few of the first inquiries financiers and lending institutions desire responded to when checking out a start-up company, and rightly so. The business plan generally attends to these and various other relevant concerns in some information, yet what concerning a Procedures Plan? If Operations is discussed at all, details are likely to be sketchy at ideal.

Does Operations Management contribute to the start-up company, and if so, what is the duty? As we explore the role of Procedures Administration in the start-up firm, we need to attend to the roles and obligations of two principals: the business owner and the procedures management specialist.

First, we need to realize the truth that Procedures might not play an essential or significant duty in a start-up firm. Procedures might play a crucial role, and when it does operations, management specialists need to be prepared. This is where the business owner or owners can be found in. It is the obligation of the entrepreneur to understand the requirements of the organization at any type of given time and the skills and experience that is require. Entrepreneurs are usually specialists in their areas and often tend to be creative "idea people" that see the big picture and can visualize the future of business. Numerous entrepreneurs have a problem with the day-to-day details of running a service, and lots of have no formal operations monitoring education and learning or experience. These entrepreneurs need to comprehend the skills that operations management experts offer the table and where and just how they fit into the start-up company (and when).

It is the obligation of the operations management professional, who is at home in the details, to adapt their abilities and knowledge to the entrepreneurial environment and to create the systems and day-to-day procedures that will help direct the company to long-term success. There are substantial differences between a fully grown, recognized organization and a start-up company, and many operations monitoring professionals might not have the abilities and experience needed to assist guide the start-up on it's meant to success. If you have really invested your profession operating in large, well developed, governmental organizations, you may be unwell prepared for life in a business organization. The rate at which decisions can be made and changes in direction can take place in a tiny or Start-up Company can be mind-boggling for those made use of bureaucracy. Thorough analysis and extensive planning are deluxe that few business owners or supervisors of start-ups can manage. Experience, sixth sense, and back of the envelope calculations typically rule the day. Procedures management professionals require to be able to adapt to this setting and have the confidence to act without the detail and assistance that they're frequently made use of to.As for the entrepreneur, exactly how do you figure out when and if you should think about a larger duty for Workflow, and just how do you tackle creating an Operations Strategy?

Well, the first thing that should be done is to recognize simply what we're talking about when we discuss Workflow and Workflow Monitoring. In a nutshell, Procedures Management worries the processes and treatments that an organization makes use of to generate their product or supply their service. Quality and client service are necessary elements that fall under the operations umbrella.

For the organization to be successful, Procedures has to have well-incorporated affiliations with all the various other functional locations, consisting of tactical planning, marketing and sales, and accountancy and finance. There has to be formal assimilation even if all of these features fall under one or just a couple of people. You have to have a sensible product or service, you require an excellent marketing method, you need funds, and you need to be able to provide the service or product. You can have a fantastic item, a constant stream of brand-new items, and interesting advertising project, and a lot of money, but if you cannot satisfy your consumers by providing the service or product with the finest quality, with the highest degree of service, you'll fall short. Delivering the services or product is in the realm of Workflow. The duty of Operations will certainly differ, of course, depending on the nature of the business and the life stage of the company.

A software program development business in the first phases of writing code will not need to pay much focus to Procedures. The company that remains in the R&D stage of integrating that software application right into elements for initial tools manufacturers requires a strong operations approach. The tool manufacturer that is at the stage of transitioning from R&D and prototyping to full production must have very developed and very comprehensive operations prepare in position if they anticipate contending in today's global marketplace. The gadget maker must have a procedure technique and plan in position from day one because operations are such a vital component of their future success. Even if it takes several years to reach the complete production mode, you should begin to create your procedures plan in the early stages of the company. You'll have a leg up on any competitors if you've developed your procedures intend and strategy as you grow, rather than waiting till you're ready to increase production. If you wait, it may already be far too late.

I've been working recently with a little contracting company. The owner approached me to assist him with his organization to prepare for a new line of work. Although I have no understanding of or experience in his market, he understands the value that Operations Management and exactly how it can assist improve his existing organization and aid get the brand-new line of business off on the ideal foot. The existing service would have taken advantage of Procedure planning and administration at earlier phases. The Procedures Management career all at once has a mainly untapped market in start-up companies in practically any market. Workflow administration specialists need to adjust their knowledge and skills to this audience. As mentioned earlier, it's a pretty sure thing to state that several, if not most, entrepreneurs do not come from a Workflow background, so what should be considered in the Operations Strategy?

The workflow includes every little thing from the procurement of the products and resources required to create the product or offer the service, with to the shipment of the product or service to the client or last consumer. The Workflow Plan has to resolve how the company will certainly do these tasks. The field of Operations Monitoring is cluttered with buzzwords (worth stream, procedure mapping), numerous systems and methods (Lean Manufacturing, Six Sigma), and three-letter acronyms (ERP, for Venture Source Preparation, generally meaning a computer system, and SCM for Supply Chain Management). The Workflow Strategy needs to puncture the mess and simply state how the organization will satisfy its customers and drive earnings.

Some aspects of the Workflow Plan to seek are:

Sourcing strategy - including supplier option requirements and provider evaluations

Quality system - just how will procedures be checked and managed? Exactly how will authority and duty for quality be designated and dispersed throughout the organization? What results are anticipated?

Production and Stock Management (applies to services and products) - where will you fulfil the customer - will you build to purchase, construct to supply, or what? What is the production and production control methodology? What are the materials and information flows?

Logistics and distribution - will warehouse and delivery solutions are performed in-house or outsourced? What are the distribution networks?

Customer service - just how much authority will be given to client service personnel? Will, there be devoted customer support employees, or will it be the obligation of operations, sales & advertising, or that? What are the assumptions for client contentment?

Assimilation - Exactly how will procedures be incorporated with the various other areas of the company?

Workflow is an essential element of every organization. The function and obligations of Procedures will vary depending upon the organization, the sector, and the life stage of the company, however the relevance will certainly not. Every organization, item manufacturer or company, for-profit or non-profit, the federal government, or personal, must effectively produce and deliver their product and services. Workflow plays a key duty in every service and needs to be offered the dedication that is required to ensure success. Every business strategy must include a comprehensive and well-established Operations Plan, and every local business owner ought to have an understanding of the function of Workflow in their company.

HOW AN ONLINE COMPANY START-UP CAN BE RECESSION RESISTANT

Circuit City shut its doors after years in the business of digital retail. A lengthy checklist of services is becoming leaner as they close stores in favour of better- doing areas. This is the company in an economic downturn. Homeowner is seeking new lessees for huge retail facilities. Very few merchants are in a placement to increase. Banks consider it risky, and the majority of sellers feel similarly. Consumers are holding a fatality grasp on their personal expenditures, and it's having a strong effect on exactly how service operates.

The Other Side of the Coin

Since finances have ended up being tighter, lots of are seeking ways to make extra money to pay for debt or pursue saving for something they need—no one such as to simply hang on when they might be able to move up. Therein exists the problem. Banks aren't in a mood to provide, so opening a basic retail company might be difficult to complete. Exactly how do you tackle creating a business with little financial investment funding and no affordable assumption for a start-up loan from your bank? The first thing you will have to do is take inventory of your readily available assets. What do you currently have that could assist you in establishing a service concept? What funds do you have available that could be utilized to launch a service?

Second, take your abilities and see how they can be incorporated into a company suggestion. By incorporating what you can do with what you have available, you can access an effective collection of tools for company advancement. Third, the business you desire might have the most effective chance of success in an internet setting. No leasing's or lease will certainly be needed, and you won't have home heating, cooling, or even constructing insurance coverage costs to fret about.

You might not also require any kind of additional staff members to make your organization strong. An online setting is outright the very least costly setting to develop the organization. It can be the most interrupted if you need to take time for meetings, college plays, or a day in the park you can do it.

Certainly your business may need your interest later on, yet if you require to live the life, you can tip far from you're on the internet shop and do it. Instead of employing a sales force, you will certainly be making use of Search Engine Optimization (SEO) to help offer your online organization. You must prepare for a number of months of lean sales. Slow sales growth is typical for any type of brand-new start-up, so patience will be crucial. Most of the abilities you will need to develop your business can be found online. It might appear frustrating; however, the, even more, you work with internet marketing strategies the much more you will begin to see just how they can adjoin and enhance each other. Discover what you have, what you can do, and then take it to the internet.

Completion outcome may be an economic downturn immune company with long-term incentives.

Exactly how to Produce a Budget Website for a Lean Launch Organisation

Getting a Launch business off the ground has actually never ever been more challenging, according to one of the most recent data, the failure price in the very first five years is as high as 80%. Think about that for a second. Of 5 individuals trying to do new business work, just one of them makes it. Spending beyond your means on start-up expenses is one of the most usual risks. And where do brand-new business owners overspend? And what product is the leading resource of unneeded investing? Company Sites. These days the internet is very affordable, so unless you plan to invest big on search engine optimization or on internet advertising, the bulk of your clients won't originate from the web. What you require as a regional launch is a website that can reveal site visitors that have already found out about you with various other methods that you have to do with.

A simple example is if you take an ad out in your neighbourhood newspaper or the yellow web pages. The ad consists of simply sufficient information to order someone's attention, and they are then informed to visit your web site to locate even more details. An expensive developer internet site with reducing- edge technology will not win over this sort of site visitor.

A straightforward, however clean site with all the crucial information will be sufficient, and with a little initiative, you can create such a website for under $500.

You want the link to be as brief as possible, but it still must give customers an idea of what you're about. If you can make it keyword rich, that is additionally a bonus offer. This is complicated as much of the most effective internet addresses are currently taken. Simply attempt to assume outside package, take your time, and even get friends and family entailed. Find yourself a site design template. Using a theme implies that you can obtain a theme that has actually been developed by a specialist with options to customize the skin with pictures (and shades) appropriate to your service. I constantly go with WordPress themes/templates. They are easy to install and make handling your content simple as well. Theme Forest has a wide variety of WordPress Templates, starting from as little as $25. Following you intend to make that theme appear relevant to your industry, and this is conveniently accomplished by adding some photos.

There is no need to go and do your own image fires (pricey!) and don't go stealing pictures from various other internet sites, and it can land you in big trouble. I stock photo has an extensive magazine of photos (actually millions), so you need to think of search terms that envelop your company. For instance, a chiropractor might browse a 'spinal column' or a child care centre may search 'toys' or 'young children' or 'children at play.' When you locate a photo, you like you do not require to purchase the big picture for the internet, utilize a tiny or medium will be ideal. The hardest component is getting the photos prepared for your WordPress layout and making any kind of small changes needed. Unless you have graphic designing experience and the called for software program, you will not have the ability to do this yourself. If you can't draw that's the penalty, simply cut the pictures up and make a collection of how you would certainly like the site to look and afterward check the image to email to your developer. In terms of getting the photos into your WordPress template, the designer might have the ability to aid you with this, or you may require to hire somebody else (or option three-view some academic video clips on WordPress and determine how to do it on your own). There is no doubt about it, creating your very own website is a lot more job, yet it will certainly lower your start-up costs. You will save hundreds of bucks and still produce an online presence to provide possible customers the information and reassurance they require to do business with you.

LEAN START-UP: SELECT THE RIGHT KIND OF WAY OF LIVING START-UP

I like info products and service organizations. I wish I would certainly have begun my entrepreneurship trip by concentrating on these two kinds of businesses. Why do first-time business owners fall short? One factor is that they try to go too BIG! They attempt to construct the next Facebook or Group on. These business owners develop businesses so complicated that they can barely explain it themselves. In this e-book, I will argue that very first-time business owners and serial business owners without success need to check out beginning information products and services.

What is the essential objective of entrepreneurship? Well, there is a myriad of reasons individuals begin businesses, but at its core, entrepreneurship has to do with generating income. The issue with consuming about the information is that you shed months and months focused on the wrong stuff. You need to be consumed about the client and just how you are most likely to market. Shortly after some specific period of time, once you have actually discovered and boosted your sales processes, perhaps

100 sales in a month-end up being simple. The takeaway right here is:

Identify exactly how in your very first month of business you can shut ten sales

Don't stress over the small details just begin?

You may be asking, but where do info services and products fit into this viewpoint? Information services and products can be sold on the First Day. Develop an eBook one early morning and start selling it that afternoon! Vomit a Facebook page for your e-book or solution to work as your web site to start.

The objective of your initial company ought to be

1) To generate income
2) To do well.

I think totally that your ideal chance to succeed is with an information item or a

B2B solution organization. Creating an information item has never ever been easier. Writing a digital book or creating a video course with iMovie is a terrific way to get going in the information items business. The margins are additionally remarkable. You produce an e-book and market it for $19. That $19 is almost pure earnings. You develop the e-book once and sell it for life! B2B solution organizations are also fast and easy to begin. Consider a service you can do for other services. Run their Twitter, Facebook, or YouTube accounts. Create a sales copy for their web site or help them, land interns. Whatever the service, it needs almost absolutely no start-up funding. The vital with both information products and services is that 1) they call for little cash to begin 2) you can begin selling on day one.

As a business owner, there is nothing much better than controlling both the product production and the sales of your product. It depends on you if the business will do well or fall short. Yes, of course, this needs a ton of operation at the beginning; however, as you find out just how to develop and market your product, you can start to induce assistance. Make sure to record every one of your processes. Prior to hiring any person, you need to know the procedure in and out. You need to have in-depth operations manual to hand the new staff member on the first day. You ought to not educate the brand-new worker directly.

RESOLVING CHALLENGES AT YOUR SITE WITH A LEAN APPROACH

Taking on Lean strategies to solve issues in medical care setups is tough for nearly any type of company. The change into a Lean company calls for significant cultural adjustments. I believe the change would be similar to transferring to a new country and needing to learn new personalized and a new language. The adjustments include the fostering of brand-new means to finding options to troubles, implementing the options, and maintaining the remedies. One attitude to adopt is the "continual quality renovation" mind-set. If you adopt this attitude, then you believe that processes and end results at your site can always be better. It's similar to the idea that you can always do even more to boost your Individual health and wellness.

Frequently doctors and supervisors assume that the waypoints work is simply great and that their site is really reliable. After that, there are those who assume outcomes could be much better yet only focus on clinical end results and those involved in professional processes. Practitioners of Lean recognize that every person and all procedures at a site are the interconnected-clinical and administrative staff, which there is constantly space for renovation. Another adjustment for a lot of websites is the way one finds options to troubles. All frequently, it is a single person or a small group of individuals who think of services to troubles. Many times, one physician or supervisor in a method determines how points will certainly be made. The various other doctors do not really want to be troubled; they just intend to deal with clients and be paid.

If you want to make significant renovations, then you need to believe that teams can solve issues better than someone, which everyone on the staff can add to solutions to problems. I am not saying that for each chance for enhancement that the whole team must be entailed. Instead, a wide depiction of the staff ought to help solve troubles; an agent from each location impacted by a procedure ought to be involved. You may wish to include some who don't seem to be involved in a procedure you are improving. They might have a concept that includes their participation, and which improves the procedure. The vital attitude for this preparation area is that the majority of troubles can be solved by tapping the experience, technology, and knowledge of the staff members. Praise to the fostering of teams to solve issues is a modification in leadership design.

A leader of trouble resolving team needs to be able to get responses from all the employees, obtain group participants to collaborate efficiently. The leader of workgroups is required not to be the same individual each time; nonetheless, a team once created should continue to have the same leader up until service for a renovation problem is discovered if another group is formed for a different problem, after that it is OK to have a brand-new leader. As the process of producing options to high quality or procedure issues will need considerable modifications for many healthcare sites, the implementation will require adjustments too. Suppose you have actually developed a plan for a new process that you believe will vastly boost some end results and eliminate some waste at your site. For instance, you have actually produced a brand-new way to hand off patients from one shift to another in a health centre ward.

What are some of the things you need to do to make the rollout of the strategy reliable? You will require to ensure that all who will be involved in the strategy understand the brand-new process. The individuals in the brand-new procedure should not only comprehend their component yet also the part to be played by others when individuals have effectively notified the devices needed for the brand-new process required to be in position. For example, a brand-new check-off sheet for patient handoff might require to be published and distributed.

When the training and supplies are in the area, a start-up time requires to be assigned. Just as a new style of management is needed for team management and the advancement of solutions to health care procedure troubles, a new technique to management is required for the execution of the solution. The leader for the present demands to be aware that the present and implementation is considerably influenced by those participating.

A leader that works well with groups will see that a registered nurse in our handoff issue might have one concept of the appropriate method to use the mark off sheet established for the process, whereas a physician who uses the sheet could have a different point of view. The factor is the leader of the turnout requirements to be aware that given that a selection of people is included, the start-up of the remedy may happen in different ways than prepared. An excellent leader will closely check the scenario and exercise the pests. A leader will certainly also lookout for those who might intend to interfere with the new procedure due to a feeling of loss of power or influence. To ensure that effective implementation of a brand-new procedure continues and that more buy into its efficiency, somebody will certainly need to collect information demonstrating positive outcomes-improved scientific end results, positive sights of those involved in the procedure, and the removal of waste (better income).

I witnessed one medical facility that made use of data to show that they had actually lowered the moment of collection for payables by over 50%. This enhanced revenue because much less initiative was required for collection for one point, and likewise, the capital boosted. The documents of the outcomes ensured the extension of the brand-new approach and likewise pointed to further opportunities for enhancement. It is critical that you define procedures to keep an eye on the results of a brand-new procedure and to find ways to tweak it. The presentation of positive end results will certainly likewise strengthen the commitment of those involved and convert those who may have been reluctant to take part.

It might be that the information shows that the brand-new procedure is even worse. Rarely will this be the case? Now you may assume that constant high quality renovation (PDSA to some) is really difficult and not worth it. New means of working in teams, new styles of leadership, issues in carrying out new procedures, and preserving the changes simply don't seem worth it. The inertia you should conquer to do well is similar to getting a patient with newly detected high blood pressure to alter his/her lifestyle. Some will change quickly; some will certainly alter slowly, and some will not change in any way and will develop more issues. Much like those that succeed in managing their hypertension, you will certainly locate that this brand-new technique to issue addressed in the healthcare atmosphere is well worth it. The data will certainly verify it.

THE FRUGAL ENTREPRENEUR: A LEAN BEGIN

Beginning your own company can produce numerous benefits and possibilities. Sadly, for most of us, these don't just fall in our lap. Typically, there are numerous challenges we need to get over along the road. One of the likely difficulties most entrepreneurs and self- beginners will certainly come across is funding. Funding will ultimately be followed by the demand to produce favourable cash flow, the lifeline of the venture. Therefore, the success of an entrepreneur is specified by his or her ability to efficiently transform/leverage readily available abilities & sources into something a lot more. You currently knew that. Right? The funding/resources part, normally, correlates to the scale of the endeavour. Thus, the bigger the task, a lot more sources, and skills are needed. This is all quite fundamental and understandable. There is one facet of resource allotment that is usually overlooked.

In a recent interview with Mr. Paul Solitario, Handling Companion at Cerium Resources LLC, I had the chance to obtain some insight right into Small Business and Entrepreneurial Funding. Mr. Solitario is rather of an expert on the subject. He has started various ventures of his own and has extensive experience in Angel Investing and encouraging. We talked about different elements of starting a business and connecting funding aspects. Most notably, Mr. Solitario discussed the topic of frugality "Frugality is incredibly vital" he preserved. According to him, thriftiness and or absence of, tells great deals about the entrepreneur and his/her concerns. It is a reputable action of how likely the venture will be to prosper. Without a doubt, frugality makes sense. This is specifically relevant for start-ups.

Thriftiness is particularly important at the beginning; however, it must be preserved throughout the life of the venture. Consider it. When feasible, why pass by residence garage over the office, push-mower over riding-mower, old PC vs. new Mac? All these totals up to excellent cost savings. The implications of saving bring a long way. Among these, you have the capacity to start on your terrific concept today, boost margins, decrease cost, and naturally come to be money positive faster.

Cash flow can be an emotionally motivating assurance of success. It is the light at the end of the passage. Also, as stated over, it is the sustenance of your venture. Applying brand-new and easily available innovations can equate to substantial savings. Take into consideration Skype for long-distance phone calls. Possibly free software such as Google or ZOHO can replace traditional but pricey office software. Depending upon what you do, there are many various other ways new modern technologies can assist you to come to be leaner.

They are very easy to locate and embrace. All of us know that adjustment is unavoidable. Why not accept it? Saving exceeds and beyond "saving paper clips."

Rather it asks for a total modification in the status quo. Saving asks to act on the important inquiry: How can we alter in a manner that really makes a lasting distinction?

It is the complete revamping of the company as usual. One easy example is to remove "that's not my job" attitude. Cross-training employees can be incredibly efficient in accomplishing this adjustment in actions. This is substantial for the majority of small companies and particularly crucial for young start-ups. Thriftiness is not unknown to you. Unfortunately, it is an underused and merely neglected practice. The idea is to remind us how wise it is to do even more with less.

How today's Entrepreneurs Make use of Constant Development

Starting an organization is one of the most exciting things you can do legitimately. The data of success are humbling. 80% of start-up services stop working in the initial five years. Having a system in a position to craft your organization is required for success. The building blocks of an organization are consumers and positive lucrative capital. Without those two things, then there is no organisation and no wide range of development.

Why is this important to me?

I constantly want to raise this concern as if I am in your shoes. I don't wish to waste your time. There are all sorts of businesses. If you are seeking to start a coffee bar or some solution-based organization that has an existing model after that, you should read the E-Myth by Michael Gerber. This publication is very useful and will assist you to systematize your company like an effective franchise business. The Lean Start-up is various. Eric is profiling companies that are trying to develop originalities and bring them to the market location.

There are two reasons that start-ups fall short, one they do not know that their clients are, and they do not recognize what the product offers. When Facebook was taking off, Mark Zuckerberg was unsure what the company was or exactly how they would certainly make money. What he was cognizant of was the network effect called Metcalf's law. The Lean Start-up consists of 3 main sections, which are all very vital. For a time, I will cover a topic under each area.

1. Vision - Vision is the property of why the organization exists. Validated learning is the name of the game. In the old days, companies had to invest a lot of capital and sources on models, design and items. They would certainly invest the majority of their capital on these undertakings and not know if individuals would really get the item. Service individuals and technology experts believe that the product needs to exist initially. This is a basic imperfection in today's rapid-paced economy. I understand people who have begun services and they were worried regarding the office space, furniture and the pipes yet not the consumer acquisition. The earnings need to precede, and the facilities can follow. If you do it the various other methods, your failing price is almost ensured.

2. Validated Learning - Instances of these would certainly be a hockey shaped curve with the time that reveals the variety of enrolments on a site or the number of mentions in PR. Every one of these things is good, yet they are not something to base decisions on for your start-up. As opposed to taking a look at advancing total amounts or gross numbers such as overall earnings and an overall number of clients, one looks at the efficiency of each team of clients that enters into contact with the item individually. Each team is called a friend.

Internet marketing people recognize this as split testing. If you are familiar with Google AdWords, after that, you can produce two ads and gauge them against each other. The most effective ad stays, and you can create a brand-new one and evaluate it versus that advertisement. This permits you to view each group separately for real outcomes. There is an old stating in service, which is - Money conceals mistakes. Friend Analytics gets rid of the blunders that Vanity stats create.

3. Disciplined Activity/ Disciplined Idea - The Lean Start-up dives pretty deep right into the production world. Examining Toyota and Ed Deming's principles yield a host of learning that can aid the start-up. Manufacturing and step- by-step development are disciplined procedures. If you dedicate to cohort analytics after that divided testing, whatever ends up being the standard?

If a software application programmer invests three months on a high-tech feature that THEY LOVE, it is really difficult to cut it out of the item if the customers do not want it. This is where the adherent and some pre-planning can help. Showing the attribute in an alpha state with a test group of clients will save the developer months of time and provide you the validated learning required to either build it or unload it. The Lean Start- up is a wonderful book that I recommend you read. If you are thinking about spending or developing a start-up, then this book is for you. These principles can be used by any business owner to create a service and validate it prior to you invest your life savings.

Below is an instance: If you assume a new item will market, you can get the supply and struck the streets. This will lead to failure. Rather you can divide examination into Google AdWords 2 items that might offer and take pre-orders prior to you spend a penny. I am on the sales and advertising side of the organization, and I can inform you it was a lot tougher before Google because you needed to knock on doors and make the calls.

CONCLUSION

Our existing economic environment agrees with ingenious start-ups.

However, there's no consensus as to the most effective strategies these businesses need to utilize to discover and maintain development.

Some managers arbitrarily try out various solutions to see what will work, developing just as many failings as they do successes. The opportunities of succeeding can be dramatically boosted just by taking a reasonable and organized method for locating the best method for running the business. The Lean Start-up is a technique to establish and take care of start-ups. Standard service techniques can be unsafe for start-ups. These organizations demand special plans and procedures for taking care of cutting-edge ventures. These policies and treatments aren't developed randomly, naturally-- they're the result of scientific strategies and research. This guide offers a methodical, scientific method for the manager to obtain the information they need to make fast decisions in today's altering world. While it might be impractical to follow this technique to the letter in every situation, executives need to leave from the guide with a fresh point of view on the troubles they face and the choices they must make.

There are many unknowns when it concerns launching a start-up. The founder has a vision, but where that vision will lead is uncertain. At first, even the item is unidentified. Markets, collaborations, and platforms-- every little thing must be sorted out. Learning is vital to the company's development. Confirmed learning is a system for showing progress in a chaotic and transforming setting. This technique has the advantage of being quick and very easy, and it's backed by empirical information chosen from real clients. Although the guide's title recommends it is geared towards start-ups, the concepts and tools are equally as beneficial for a bigger business. Established companies can unlock the development capacity of advancement, yet to do so, they'll need to make some mindful modifications in business culture. Start-ups might benefit from having top cutting-edge qualities already built right into their cultures. However, older companies can catch up.

CPSIA information can be obtained
at www.ICGtesting.com
Printed in the USA
BVHW042002140423
662364BV00009B/560